BRITISH AR
THE RHINE

THE BAOR, 1945–1993

PAUL CHRYSTAL

Pen & Sword
MILITARY

For WOII (RQMS) Eric Wright Chrystal and Major David Chrystal

Eric Chrystal, shortly before the battle of Arnhem, where he was taken PoW,
September 1944.

First published in Great Britain in 2018 by
PEN AND SWORD MILITARY
an imprint of
Pen and Sword Books Ltd
47 Church Street
Barnsley
South Yorkshire S70 2AS

Copyright © Paul Chrystal, 2018

ISBN 978 1 526728 53 1

Typeset by Aura Technology and Software Services, India
Printed and bound by CPI Group (UK) Ltd, Croydon, CR0 4YY

Pen & Sword Books Ltd incorporates the imprints of Pen & Sword
Archaeology, Atlas, Aviation, Battleground, Discovery, Family History, History, Maritime, Military,
Naval, Politics, Railways, Select, Social History, Transport, True Crime, Claymore Press, Frontline
Books, Leo Cooper, Praetorian Press, Remember When, Seaforth Publishing and Wharncliffe.

For a complete list of Pen and Sword titles please contact
Pen and Sword Books Limited
47 Church Street, Barnsley, South Yorkshire, S70 2AS, England
email: enquiries@pen-and-sword.co.uk
website: www.pen-and-sword.co.uk

Front cover photo: A Challenger 2 main battle tank from the Royal Scots Dragoon Guards at Bergen
Hohne, Germany. (MoD)
Back cover photo: 'Across the wire'. (David Budnik / Library of Congress)

CONTENTS

ABBREVIATIONS

2ATAF	Second Allied Tactical Air Force
APC	armoured personnel carrier
BAFO	British Air Forces of Occupation
BAOR	British Army of the Rhine
BFBS	British Forces Broadcasting Service
BFES	British Families Education Service
BFN	British Forces Network
BFR	British Forces Radio
BMH	British Military Hospital
CCG (BE)	Control Commission Germany (British Element)
CFE	Canadian Forces Europe
CIBG	Canadian Infantry Brigade Group
COS	(British) Chiefs of Staff
CSDIC	Combined Services Detailed Interrogation Centre
CSEU	Combined Services Entertainment Unit
ERP	European Recovery Programme
FRG	Federal Republic of Germany
GARIOA	Government Aid and Relief in Occupied Areas
GDR	German Democratic Republic
GSO	German Service Organization
IGB	Inner German Border
INLA	Irish National Liberation Army
IRA	Irish Republican Army
IWM	Imperial War Museum
JOC	Joint Operations Centre
JSLO	Joint Services Liaison Officer
MAD	mutually assured destruction
MCTG	Mobile Civilian Transport Group
MSO	Mixed Service Organization
NA	National Archives
NAAFI	Navy, Army and Air Force Institutes
NATO	North Atlantic Treaty Organization
NCO	non-commissioned officer

NORTHAG	Northern Army Group
NRW	North Rhine-Westphalia (Nordrhein Westfalen)
POW	prisoner of war
RAF	Royal Air Force
RAFG	Royal Air Force Germany
RASC	Royal Army Service Corps
RCAF	Royal Canadian Air Force
REME	(The Corps of) Royal Electrical and Mechanical Engineers
RM	Royal Marines
RN	Royal Navy
SFA	service family accommodation
SKC	Services Kinema Corporation
SSVC	Services Sound and Vision Corporation
TA	Territorial Army
TAF	Tactical Air Force

A woman weeps on a mass grave on the first anniversary of the liberation of Bergen-Belsen concentration camp, April 1946. (Sgt R. Makin, No 5 Army Film & Photographic Unit / IWM)

AUTHOR'S NOTE

"These were huge armies that we were going to have to take on, and we were inevitably going to be overwhelmed by numbers. Therefore it was [about] an amount of damage that we could do ... to limit their advance, before nuclear release, before we actually used tactical nuclear weapons."

Maj-Gen Patrick Cordingley, former CO 7th Armoured Brigade, puts the role of the BAOR in a nutshell, *Forces News*, 2014

This book forms part of the Pen & Sword series on the Cold War which takes in the main theatres of that 'war', ranging from Aden and Kenya to Korea and Vietnam, from Malaya, Cuba and Cyprus to Suez and West Germany. The West German element—BAOR—has been relatively neglected until now, despite its pivotal position on the front line, facing the massed forces of the Russians and East Germans assembled close by behind the Iron Curtain. Colonel P. V. Panton OBE, CO 1st Battalion The Queen's Regiment and subsequently the regimental secretary of The Princess of Wales's Royal Regiment, was absolutely right when he asserts in his illuminating article on four tours with the BAOR between 1960 and 1980: "It has often struck me that very little has ever been written about the British Army of the Rhine. Much has quite rightly been written about warfare and the endless series of operations that the Army has been involved in over the post-World War II years, but all the years of the so-called Cold War, keeping the peace between NATO and the Soviet bloc, have really received very little coverage. There are whole generations of us soldiers who were weaned on the Soviet threat, who spent many years of our military service preparing for World War III in Germany, and much of whose training and way of life was bound up in numerous postings to BAOR and the almost surreal existence that it entailed."

This book goes some way in correcting this omission: it describes the Germany in which British troops found themselves from 1945 and the attitudes which prevailed among British and Germans during the Cold War years. It also provides a survey of the Cold War as played out by British troops on the northern plains and hills of what was then West Germany and in the independent British sector of Berlin. The BAOR served across 129 different locations, not including the bases used by the RAF, Royal Navy and Royal Marines during the period. The hugely expensive, long-term stationing of troops in West Germany was just one way in which the British government invested massive amounts of time and money in the political, military and economic

The GDR was eager to paint itself as a thriving, healthy regime, as seen by this wholesome farmworker in 1980. (Benno Bartocha / Bundesarchiv)

rehabilitation of a resurging Germany—other resources going into helping to secure Marshall Aid, helping to establish NATO and the Western European Union, laying the foundations for a new German sovereign state and providing military support and humanitarian aid during the Berlin blockade. All of this in the face of a by and large anti-German public both back home and among BAOR personnel, a German-phobic British press and an ambivalent Germany.

The nervous and edgy political tension between East and West, the Cold War, started to emerge before the end of the Second World War and lasted until 1994 with the earlier collapse of the Soviet Union. The (second) British Army of the Rhine was born in 1945 out of the British Liberation Army at the close of the war and took on the role of military government of the British zone of occupied Germany. It was, in effect, an army of occupation, charged with bringing order out of many levels and layers of chaos and confusion caused by massive population displacement, ethnic cleansing on an industrial scale, floods of refugees and internecine political activists intent on revenge, justice and on establishing themselves as top powers in various parts of Europe. At the same time, confrontation between the Soviets and western allies looked increasingly inevitable.

The Paris Peace Conference of May 1952 changed the political, military and socio-economic landscapes, making West Germany a sovereign nation and ending

The GDR attempted to portray itself as a modern, international state. These four fashionistas pose in Leipzig, 1972. (Ulrich Hassler / Bundesarchiv)

BAOR's role as an army of occupation. West Germany had swiftly changed from enemy to ally. The British were in Germany henceforth by invitation of the German government, not by dint of their victory in World War II. As the menacing Soviet threat increased, so BAOR assumed the role of one of the key defenders of Western Europe, and a major player in NATO after 1949. It was now BAOR'S task to integrate Germany, an eventually rearmed Germany, into an economic and military alliance to enforce the strength and military capability of Western Europe and thus forge a Europe better equipped to face down the Warsaw Pact threat from the east. This book traces and examines the changing and challenging role of the BAOR from 1945 to its demise following the 1993 'Options for Change' defence cuts.

Military and geopolitical matters are obviously paramount here, but they are only part of the story. Postings to units within the BAOR were 'accompanied', meaning that families followed the soldiers and airmen to all the stations and bases (Operation Union), from Rheindalen and Iserlohn to Minden and Berlin, from Paderborn and Hohne to Gütersloh and Lemgo. The establishment of this army involved much more than the deployment and training of troops in West Germany: entire fully functioning communities had to be created involving services and facilities not just for the servicement but for their wives, partners and children too. Dependants were as much part of the BAOR as the servicemen and -women although it is unlikely that the wives saw themselves as such. Their presence meant married quarters, schools, hospitals, GP medical centres, shops (NAAFIs and Toc H), churches, entertainment and other essential provision and social care, advice and facilities (HIVEs). This book looks at the BAOR in its entirety and surveys the social as well as the military.

Essentially, it examines the part the BAOR played in the defence of West Germany, its effectiveness as a Cold War deterrent, the garrisons and capabilities, logistics and infrastructure, its arms and armour, the nuclear option and the lives of the thousands servicemen and their families living on the front line in Germany.

INTRODUCTION

The BAOR we know from the aftermath of World War II was, in fact the second of two BAORs. The first was established in March 1919 to facilitate the British occupation of the Rhineland under the terms of the November 1918 armistice. The British were joined by the occupying armies of the United States of America, Belgium, and France. The British army initially comprised five corps, composed of two divisions each, plus a cavalry division. It went into Germany on 3 December 1918 and was established as the occupying force in March 1919. BAOR was headquartered at Cologne. *The Cologne Post* was their publication, published from 31 March 1919 to 17 January 1926.

By August 1920 the BAOR comprised approximately 13,360 troops, consisting of staff, cavalry, Royal Artillery, Royal Engineers, infantry, machine-gun corps, tanks, and the usual ancillary services. The troops were mainly located around Cologne at an approximate cost of £300,000 per month.

A group of BAOR officers of the Queen Mary's Army Auxiliary Corps, in the charge of Mrs Gladys Maud Feiling, working under the Deputy Provost Marshal, Cologne, 1919. (Ernest Brooks / IWM)

British army signallers practise semaphore and the heliograph at one of the Rhine bridges. Cologne, 23 April 1919. (John Warwick Brooke / IWM)

When asked in the House of Commons the total cost for the British Army of Occupation on the Rhine during the twelve months ending 30 June 1923 and the amount of reparations received by Great Britain during the same period, the reply from Sir W. Joynson-Hicks was: "The total cost of the British Army of Occupation on the Rhine during the twelve months ended 30th June, 1923, was £1,740,000 (exclusive of accommodation and miscellaneous services provided free by Germany). Of this amount, £350,645 was covered by paper Marks supplied by the German Government to meet local expenditure, so that the net cost was about £1,380,000. The amount received by the Treasury on account of cost of occupation and reparation during the same period, apart from the paper mark receipts referred to above, was £8,287,000."

The British Army left Germany in 1929 and BAOR was disbanded only to be revived fifteen years later in the hectic and chaotic aftermath of World War II. The British Army of the Rhine we associate with the Cold War, as stationed in many parts of West Germany, in the British sector, has its origins in 1943 with the creation of 21st Army Group which was tasked with the invasion of Europe (Operation Overlord) in 1944. Formed in September 1943 in England and led by General (later Field Marshal) Sir Bernard Montgomery, it initially controlled all ground forces in Operation Overlord but as soon as enough American forces had landed, they formed their own 12th Army Group under General Omar Bradley; 21st Army Group was left with the British Second Army and the First Canadian Army.

After the Normandy landings, units of 21st Army Group eventually crossed the Rhine near Wesel on 23 March 1945. Despite intense resistance, British, Canadian and American units advanced into the German *Länder* (states) of Nordrhein-Westfalen, Niedersachsen and Schleswig-Holstein, thus paving the way for the British Army's occupation of the north of the defeated country and establishing what became the British zone with troops often based in various former Wehrmacht barracks.

The February 1945 Yalta Conference, as ratified in part at the July 1945 Potsdam Conference, agreed that Germany be divided into four main zones along with a small French zone on the Franco-German border. Similar divisions were agreed for Austria and the City of Berlin in East Germany in the Russian zone of occupation. The earlier transfer of East Prussia and the move of the border between Germany and Poland to the Oder–Neisse Line were unaffected.

21st Army Group was established from the British Liberation Army and redesignated the 'British Army of the Rhine' three months after the end of the war on 25 August 1945. Initially it comprised 77,000 men. British Liberation Army (BLA) was the official name given to the British forces that fought from the Normandy invasion to end of the war. Most BLA units were assigned to the 21st Army Group, which also included forces from other countries. Montgomery in a message to the troops said, "Although our name is changed we are still the same." HQ was in the pleasant spa town of Bad Oeynhausen and consisted of one Guards division, three armoured divisions, seven infantry divisions, 1st Polish Armoured Division and 3rd Canadian Infantry Division, CAOF. The 77,000 comprised sixteen armoured regiments and 21 battalions of infantry in four divisions. But the total number of British implicated in the BAOR on the North German Plain in whatever capacity was nearer 200,000, including the troops and support staff in Berlin numbering some 30,000 plus the RAF; we should not forget the schoolteachers, doctors, dentists, nurses, welfare staff, Salvation Army, Toc H and NAAFI staff. Postings to Germany got longer, in some cases with infantry regiments staying for five years and armoured regiments longer. The Queen's Royal Irish Hussars were in Paderborn for nine years in the 1970s.

BAOR's original function was to control the corps districts which were running the military government of the British zone of occupied Germany. After German civilians took over the running of civil government, it became the command formation for the troops in Germany only, rather than being responsible for civil administration as well.

The BAOR served across some 129 different locations in the British zone of occupation during its existence, excluding the bases used by the RAF, Royal Navy and Royal Marines during the period. When NATO came together in 1949, BAOR constituted the British land force contribution based at Bielefeld. 29 November 1952 saw the formation of the Headquarters of Northern Army Group (NORTHAG), a NATO creation under whose command BAOR was placed. Significantly, BAOR, along with Belgian, Canadian, and Dutch army units, now elided from an occupation force into taking pro-active responsibility for NORTHAG's northern front from Hamburg to Kassel to counter a Soviet invasion from Russia and the seven Soviet satellite states of Central and Eastern Europe, the forces of what was later to become the Warsaw Pact of 1955. In October 1954, HQ BAOR had relocated from Bad Oeynhausen to Rheindalen.

In 1956 major changes to the BAOR started to make it look like the army with which we are familiar. Brigade groups took over from divisions with a brigade group comprising armour, infantry, an engineer (REME) squadron and an armoured reconnaissance regiment, compared with divisions comprising just of infantry and armour. The BAOR now consisted of three main elements: the main force of I (BR) Corps HQ'd at Bielefeld; the British Rear Combat Zone headquartered in Düsseldorf, responsible for logistics and the resupply of the combat formations; the British Communications Zone HQ at Emblem, Belgium whose job it was to receive reinforcements from the UK as required and to coordinate their onward deployment to I (BR) Corps. Finally, there was the Berlin Infantry Brigade, a 3,000-strong force independent of and not subordinated to NORTHAG but under the control of the Allied Control Council in Berlin.

40 Signals Regiment training with a Sea King helicopter. (David Chrystal)

Under a camouflage net with SA 80s. (David Chrystal)

Every Germany-based unit was required to have 85 percent of personnel on station and ready at all times. For good reason: at this time, the USSR had as many as 60 divisions based in East Germany.

Additional support for I (BR) Corps came from the 2nd Infantry Division at Catterick, on standby to deploy at a moment's notice. The 24th Airmobile Brigade was also part of the division, fully air portable and on standby for transportation by helicopter complete with equipment. The three infantry battalions were tasked with anti-armour operations.

Cuts began in 1957 when BAOR was reduced by 20 percent from 80,000 to 64,000. National service came to an end between 1958 and 1960, forcing further reductions to 55,000 men and the restructuring of the BAOR into three divisions of two armoured brigade groups and five infantry brigade groups. Then, in 1963, seven brigade groups were reformed into three central divisions.

In January 1963 John Profumo, secretary of state for war, told the House that, "The tactical nuclear weapons available to the British Army in Germany are 8-inch howitzers, Honest John rockets and Corporal guided weapons." The Challenger took over from the Centurion as the main battle tank; it was the British Army of the Rhine's tank of choice in formulating strategy for defensive operations against Soviet and Warsaw Pact forces in Germany.

BAOR participated endlessly in various exercises such as 'Reforger' or 'Return of Forces to Germany' alongside the United States and other NATO armies to ensure its total readiness in time of a crisis. Units of the Territorial Army (TA) also carried out exercises across West Germany. Various other reshuffles took place over the decades, endlessly balancing armour with infantry and infantry with armour. BAOR was continually reduced, restructured and re-equipped with new matériel. Over the years of its existence the strength of the BAOR fluctuated between 60,000 and 25,000 troops commanded by a four-star general from headquarters at Rheindahlen, which also housed the headquarters of RAF Germany, NORTHAG and 2nd Allied Tactical Air Force.

Finally, in 1992 when the Soviet Union evaporated, I British Corps was disbanded to be replaced by Allied Command Europe Rapid Reaction Corps (ARRC), part of NATO. This development, and the 'Options for Change' plan, were indicative of the future for the British army in Germany in the wake of the apparent reduction of overt threat levels from the USSR. Recent events in the Crimea and in the Ukraine throw that decision into some doubt.

Units from the BAOR were regularly deployed to operate under UN command as part of BATT and UN peacekeeping operations and, during the Northern Ireland

A member of 34 Squadron, RAF Regiment, taking cover in a defensive position after coming under fire from 'enemy forces' during a late afternoon patrol. The RAF personnel were conducting air traffic operations and force protection during Exercise Volcanex at a fictional deployed operating base in southern Germany. (MoD)

Troubles, they also took part in regular deployments to Northern Ireland for tours of three or six months.

Had war broken out in West Germany, the BAOR would have come under NATO command. BAOR as I (BR) Corps would have been tasked to defend a sector of the North German Plain as part of Armed Forces Central Europe (AF CENT). BAOR formed part of Northern Army Group (NORTHAG) as part of AF CENT and NORTHAG and would be partnered by the Central Army Group. NORTHAG's operational area extended from Hamburg down to Kassel and from the Netherlands border to the Inner German border (Iron Curtain) with communist East Germany.

Within NORTHAG, BAOR had I Netherlands Corps to the far north, I German Corps to the immediate north, and I Belgium Corps in the south. The I British Corps area extended just north of Hanover down to just north of Kassel, and extended from the inner German border to a line west of Soest, but the BAOR boundary itself extended right back to Antwerp in Belgium. In the event of war, BAOR would become British Support Command, which would supply I British Corps and guard the rear areas. The strategy was that if I (BR) Corps' area was threatened, the corps would fight with two of its armoured divisions forward-deployed with one left in reserve. When the 2nd Infantry Division arrived it would defend vital military targets in the corps rear; 24th Airmobile Brigade would be ready to counter any rapid enemy armoured thrust.

But, as already noted, BAOR was never just about regiments, squadrons, airmen and soldiers. There was a substantial civilian presence in the zone with families and dependents living on family 'patches' around the barracks. The quarters, NAAFIs, Toc Hs, Hives, cinemas, messes, BFBS, BFPO, day and boarding schools, and military hospitals all ensured a comfortable way of life and good standard of living that was a mirror image, albeit a generally more prosperous mirror image, of life back home, but with the added bonus of easy travel to neighbouring countries, some quite stunning scenery, beautiful towns and villages and the opportunity, if desired, to imbibe a new culture and language from, at least after a rather mutually frigid few early years, a welcoming and warm native population.

With the end of the Cold War and subsequent reunification of Germany, BAOR was officially disbanded on 28 October 1994. BAOR was succeeded by British Forces Germany, which also incorporates the former RAF Germany.

The British sector in Berlin was always a separate entity from the BAOR. From November 1946 after the allied division of the city, the British garrison comprised an armoured squadron and two infantry battalions, increasing to three in 1948. This all went under the name British Troops Berlin, later in 1949 as Area Troops Berlin. Various other reincarnations followed with alarming regularity in 1953, 1959, 1963 and 1977 until in 1981 it was rebadged Berlin Infantry Brigade for a second time. An air defence troop was added in 1986 at which point the brigade was some 3,100 strong. Gradual reductions came during 1992/3 and it was disbanded in 1994.

1. COLD WAR

The BAOR was inseparable from the Cold War. Essentially, the Cold War was a period of geopolitical tension extending from soon after World War II, around 1947, to the fall of the Soviet Union and the Warsaw Pact, as symbolized by the dismantling of the Berlin Wall in 1991. Forty-six years, then, of tense stand-off between Russia and her allies, and the US and her allies, including Britain. The British armed forces in the guise of the BAOR were at the forefront of what is probably the longest conflict-free military confrontation in history, stationed as it was on the front line facing the serried ranks of the East German and Soviet armies. The BAOR operated from their military bases in what was West Germany and in the British sector of West Berlin, 125 miles deep in the Soviet zone. The BAOR trained endlessly in their extensive training grounds on the North German Plain.

The Cold War was a product of and a consequence of World War II. Soon after the Russian army dramatically broke out of the besieged city of Stalingrad in February 1943, defeated the German Sixth Army and began its relentless and victorious march to Berlin, the allied leaders, Stalin, Roosevelt and Churchill, sat down together to discuss how the world was to be shaped in the wake of an expected allied victory. Recent history of the nations involved, concerns about the political and military future, economics and ideology all had compelling parts to play in the objectives and wishes of each of the leaders. Clearly, it was never going to be a simple, congenial and straightforward discussion and it was probably obvious at the first of their three major meetings between the three in Tehran from 28 November to 1 December 1943, after the Anglo-Soviet Invasion of Iran, that compromise was going to have to feature heavily, both in the final agreement and in initial relationships and conduct after the eventual ceasefire. The Soviet position was always very clear, as they demonstrated at Tehran: they were intent on delimiting the opportunity for Germany to re-emerge as an industrial-cum -military power that was capable of threatening Russia again; stripping Germany of what was left of its industrial base would achieve this as well as helping to restore the decimated Soviet industrial infrastructure through the deconstruction of German factories and transporting them for reconstruction back in Russia. The US vacillated over whether to take a punitive stance and emasculate Germany completely, or to invest in Germany to enable her to participate constructively in the restoration of post-war Europe.

Something approaching sixty million people lost their lives as a result of World War II, two-thirds of them civilians. The Axis powers of Germany, Italy and Japan incurred three million civilian deaths; but the Allies suffered thirty-five million civilian deaths. In the Soviet Union, Poland and Yugoslavia this amounted to a staggering 10–20 percent of the total populations; in Italy, Austria, Hungary, China and Japan between 4 and 6 percent of the total populations lost their lives. Germany saw 6.9 to 7.5 million Germans killed, between 8.26 and 8.86 percent of the population.

To give some idea of the immediate post-war carnage and chaos we can look at Russia, a country three times the size of the US, and covering a sixth of the earth's land mass. The Soviets lost twenty-five million dead, twenty-five million were reduced to homelessness, six million buildings were destroyed; farmsteads were destroyed; the Russian industrial base and 31,000 of its factories were devastated courtesy of the Germans; 65,000 kilometres of railway track were wrecked. Every Russian family was touched by death, be it combatant or civilian; over one million lives were lost at Leningrad alone; 1,700 cities and towns snd 70,000 villages were totally wrecked. Nine of the fifteen Soviet republics were occupied by the Germans who raped, murdered and pillaged at will. Small wonder then that the Russian leadership was determined to ensure that their homeland never had to endure anything like this again. Poland was particularly sensitive: the Polish corridor had been the access route used for the invasion of Russia by Hitler in 1941; but he was by no means the first: Napoleon and the Kaiser had both passed through before. The future of Poland and its deployment as a counter-German buffer zone then was vital to Soviet security.

Apart from bestriding the globe and involving many countries in Europe, Asia, the Americas, the Middle East and Africa, the Cold War significantly saw the two protagonists, the USSR and the US, at loggerheads with each other in every conceivable respect. Their essential differences in economy, ideology and the other factors enumerated above opened the door for espionage and counter-espionage, propaganda, psychological warfare, destabilization, rivalry in sport and a space race. But, from the very start, the bottom line was always the nuclear capability enjoyed by the US and, eventually, the USSR. The threat offered by both to initiate a nuclear world war and the need to defend robustly against such a nightmare scenario forever kept the fires of the Cold War burning. Ironically and paradoxically, the very real threat, or promise, of mutually assured destruction (MAD) kept the world safe. Nowhere was this irony or paradox clearer than on the border separating the two Germanys, with their armies poised on either side of the Iron Curtain. No army was more aware of its pivotal role deterring, defending against or retaliating against a nuclear or conventional attack than the British Army of the Rhine.

The brittle glue bonding the three powers during wartime—the common aim to annihilate Nazi Germany—soon fell away after the ceasefire of May 1945. Mutual suspicion had characterized this fragile alliance of convenience and so it was after peace was signed: despite the obvious benefits of the US's Lend-Lease Program to Russia and Britain, despite the $11 billion-plus in military aid to the Soviets by the

US to ensure the survival of Russia in the face of German aggression intent on grabbing the Soviet's mineral wealth, a paranoid Stalin was highly suspicious, believing that the British and the Americans had conspired to burden the Soviet Union with a disproportionate amount of the fighting against the Nazis. The Western Allies, he believed, had intentionally dragged their feet on opening a second front to relieve the pressure on Soviet forces so that they might show up at the last minute and influence and shape the peace negotiations to their own advantage. The invasion of Normandy was repeatedly postponed, Russia was responsible in 1943 and 1944 for tying down 80 percent of Wehrmacht divisions, and invaded Russia did not enjoy the luxury of picking and choosing when to commit her armies against the Germans. Machiavellianism was up and running well before the war ended with Stalin setting up training camps in eastern European countries for communists so that they could establish secret police units loyal to Moscow as soon as the Red Army took control. Soviet agents appropriated the media; they banned all civic institutions, from innocuous youth groups to innocuous schools, churches and rival political parties.

During their push toward Berlin the Soviets paused before Warsaw where a Polish uprising attempted to claim the capital. The Germans poured into the city and exterminated the resistance with the Soviets refusing access to Soviet airfields to Allied air power and refusing to intervene to help the Poles. In sixty-three days of slaughter the Nazis slew 200,000 Poles, mostly civilians, while the Russians stood by. This slaughter severely depleted the Polish resistance and would facilitate the takeover of the country after the war—the first plank in the Russian buffer zone strategy.

However, if Stalin needed justification for his paranoia he got it in spades when, toward the end of the war, Roosevelt insulted Stalin by negotiating a separate peace with SS General Karl Wolff in northern Italy. The Soviet Union was excluded and Roosevelt and Stalin exchanged angry words. Wolff, a war criminal, was guaranteed immunity at the Nuremberg trials by Office of Strategic Services (OSS) commander and later CIA director Allen Dulles when they met in March 1945. The US was considering enlisting Wolff and his forces to help implement 'Operation Unthinkable', basically a secret plan for victorious US and defeated Germany to invade the Soviet Union, a plan which Winston Churchill advocated.

'Operation Unthinkable' was the codename for two plans by the Western Allies against the Soviet Union ordered by Churchill: the first was a surprise attack on Soviet armies in Germany with the aim to "impose the will of the Western Allies" on the Soviets. This 'will' was qualified as a "square deal for Poland" which meant enforcing the recently signed Yalta agreement. When this was judged "fanciful", the plan was abandoned, only to be replaced by a defensive scenario, in which the British were to defend against a Soviet drive toward the North Sea and the Atlantic following the withdrawal of American forces from Europe.

The Warsaw uprising: Polish fighters in the region of Kredytowa-Królewska Street. (Jerzy Piorkowski)

'Unthinkable' was the first Cold War-era contingency plan for war with the Soviet Union. Both plans were top secret and it was not until 1998 that they were declassified; it is likely, however, that Guy Burgess passed some details to the Soviets at the time.

With Germany on the verge of defeat there was now no common purpose among the Allies. The Yalta Conference was held from 4 to 11 February 1945, convened to air and iron out the significant differences each of the powers had over security going forward, and to agree on a plan to provide the liberated populations of post-Nazi Europe with self-determination.

Each of the three leaders vigorously pushed for their own agendas: Roosevelt wanted Soviet support against Japan, specifically for a planned invasion of Japan—Operation August Storm—as well as Soviet participation in the United Nations; Churchill urged free elections and democratic governments in Eastern and Central Europe, notably Poland; and Stalin demanded substantial reparations from Germany and insisted on Soviet influence in Eastern and Central Europe, not least in Poland, as a vital aspect of the USSR's national security strategy. It is worth noting that at this time the Red Army occupied Poland completely and held much of Eastern Europe with a military power three times greater than Allied forces in the West.

Here is a summary of the main Yalta agreements: the unconditional surrender of Nazi Germany was the priority; post-war, Germany and Berlin would be split into four occupied zones; Stalin agreed that France have a fourth occupation zone in Germany, formed from the American and British zones; Germany would undergo demilitarization and denazification; German reparations were partly to be in the form of forced labour to be used to repair damage that Germany had inflicted on its victims; in all, Germany was to pay $20 billion in reparations, half ring-fenced for the Soviet Union (subject to later confirmation); it was agreed to reorganize the communist Provisional Government of the Republic of Poland that had been installed by the Soviet Union in Lublin "on a broader democratic basis" (the Polish government in exile in London was rejected); the Polish eastern border would follow the Curzon Line, and Poland would receive territorial compensation in the west from Germany; Stalin pledged to allow free elections in Poland; Roosevelt obtained a commitment from Stalin to participate in the UN; Stalin agreed to enter the war against Japan "in two or three months after Germany has surrendered and the war in Europe is terminated", and that as a result, the Soviets would take possession of southern Sakhalin and the Kuril islands, the port of Dalian would be internationalized, and the Soviet lease of Port Arthur would be restored, among other concessions; Nazi war criminals were to be hunted down and put on trial; democracies would be established, and all liberated European and former Axis satellite countries would hold free elections and order would be restored.

By March, however, things had started to unravel and it was clear that the Soviets were reneging on their promises in relation to Poland and discarding the democratic processes underpinning the deal as established in the Declaration on Liberated Europe. Soviet repression of non-communist Poles and the Red Army's cavalier and bullying treatment of Hungary, Romania and Bulgaria added to the concern felt by Roosevelt and Churchill over the Soviet interpretation of the Yalta accord. Roosevelt's ambassador to the USSR, Averell Harriman, cabled Roosevelt that "we must come clearly to realize that the Soviet program is the establishment of totalitarianism, ending personal liberty and democracy as we know it". Two days later, Roosevelt admitted that his opinion of Stalin had been somewhat over- optimistic. The Poles, understandably, felt deserted and realized that their allies had sold them down the river despite the incalculable contribution they had made to the defeat of Germany: over 200,000 soldiers of the Polish Armed Forces in the West were serving in the British army toward the end of the war.

Roosevelt died suddenly and was replaced by the less flexible Harry S. Truman who wasted no time in reminding the Soviet foreign minister, V. M. Molotov, of his Yalta obligations to Polish democracy. The elections of 1947 were preceded by the systematic incarceration, kidnapping and elimination of troublesome pro-Western activists enabling the communists to claim 80 percent of the vote. Romania and Bulgaria espoused communism, aided no doubt by Soviet infiltration; northern Iran fell to the Russians and the Soviet state of Azerbaijan was established; Russian troops massed along the border with Turkey.

Clearly, Russia and the US wasted no time in firmly establishing their respective post-war positions with the former exerting its influence over and consolidating its control over the states of the Eastern Bloc, while the latter responded by opposing the build-up of Soviet power by extending military and financial aid—the Marshall Plan delivered $13 billion to the countries of Western Europe between 1948 and 1952—and helping to establish the NATO alliance. The Soviets and the Americans had very different ideas about how to bring about security for their respective countries. To the Soviets it was simply a question of suppressing or eliminating opposition, spreading influence by exerting control; the objectives exercised by the US were much the same, except that their methods were perhaps less overt and more diplomatic.

West Berlin, Germany. Marshall Plan aid to Germany, 1949.

The Potsdam Conference was held from July to August 1945, involving Clement Attlee who had replaced Churchill as prime minister and Truman. Here, the Soviets refuted accusations that they were interfering in the internal affairs of Romania, Bulgaria and Hungary. The conference brought about the Potsdam Declaration regarding the surrender of Japan, and the Potsdam Agreement ratifying to some extent the planned Soviet regime in Poland, the annexation of former Polish territory east of the Curzon Line, and, provisions for the annexation of parts of Germany east of the Oder–Neisse line into Poland, and northern East Prussia into the Soviet Union. The $10 billion reparations were now a stumbling block because the US had decided to support an industrially resurgent Germany and reparations would only impede that renaissance. Furthermore, the negative impact and hideous repercussions reparations had created after World War I signalled caution. The matter was, on the surface at least, resolved by the US, USSR, France and the UK agreeing to extract reparations individually from their own zones of occupation.

The bungled and fudged Polish question and the more pugnacious attitude of the three powers at Potsdam would characterize the hostile relationship, the entrenchment and the one-upmanship and inflexibility which persisted for the duration of the Cold War. It was at Potsdam that Truman chose to tell Stalin about the United States' shiny, new, powerful weapon.

To Stalin in 1946 the writing was very much on the wall: another war was inevitable because "the development of world capitalism proceeds not along the path of smooth and even progress but through crisis and the catastrophes of war". This caused alarm in Washington and led to George Kennan's 8,000-word 'Long Telegram' in response, which in turn helped shape US policy going forward: the policy of containment. The alarm was heightened later that year when the Soviets initially showed no interest in withdrawing its troops from northern Iran, thus threatening the West's oil supplies. In March 1946 former prime minister Churchill made his famous apocalyptic pronouncement: "From Stettin in the Baltic to Trieste in the Adriatic, an iron curtain has descended across the continent."

Division then was the future, championed by the US and the UK: the possibility of a reunified Germany which may in the future ally with Russia, or even a neutral Germany in a no-man's land abutting an increasingly powerful Soviet Union, was not an option. Things would first come to a head with a disgruntled Soviet Union's blockade of Berlin of 1948/9 and the resulting airlift.

To some extent the Soviet consolidation of its control over the states of the Eastern Bloc was the resumption of unfinished business which had begun at the start of World War II. An agreement with Nazi Germany in the Molotov–Ribbentrop Pact allowed the Soviet annexation of eastern Poland incorporated into two separate Soviet socialist republics; Latvia, Estonia, Lithuania; part of eastern Finland which became the

Karelo-Finnish SSR, and eastern Romania which became the Moldavian SSR. Post-war, these were complemented by the People's Republic of Albania (11 January 1946), People's Republic of Bulgaria (15 September 1946), People's Republic of Poland (19 January 1947), People's Republic of Romania (13 April 1948), Czechoslovak Socialist Republic (9 May 1948), Hungarian People's Republic (20 August 1949) and German Democratic Republic (7 October 1949).

So, the scene was more or less set with the Soviets consolidating their power east of the GDR border and the British and US similarly entrenched to the west of the border with a sector in partitioned Berlin.

The Berlin blockade saw the Soviet Union block the Western Allies' access to railway, road, and canal in the sectors of Berlin under Western control. This action was in preference to another option open to the Soviets: deploying tanks to surround the city. The Soviets would only lift the blockade if the Western Allies agreed to withdraw the newly introduced B-mark deutschemark from West Berlin, a fiscal measure

US Navy Douglas R4D and US Air Force C-47 aircraft unload at Tempelhof Airport during the Berlin airlift. The first aircraft is a C-47A-90-DL (s/n 43-15672).

seen as a key factor in the industrial and economic resurrection of a partitioned Germany. In response, the Western Allies instigated the Berlin airlift (26 June 1948–30 September 1949) to deliver supplies to the two million people of besieged West Berlin. Aircrews from the United States Air Force, the British Royal Air Force, the French Air Force, the Royal Canadian Air Force, the Royal Australian Air Force, the Royal New Zealand Air Force, and the South African Air Force flew over 200,000 sorties in one year, providing the West Berliners up to 8,893 tons of supplies every day, mainly fuel and food. The Soviets did not intervene in the airlift lest this might lead to conflict. By April 1949, the airlift was delivering more cargo than had previously been transported into the city by rail. On 12 May 1949, the USSR lifted the blockade.

A failure by any definition and public relations disaster with global repercussions, the immediate outcome of the blockade was the establishment by the West of the Federal Republic of Germany and, in response, the German Democratic Republic by the Soviets. 4 April 1949 saw the landmark establishment of NATO "to keep the Americans in, the Soviets out and the Germans down". A mutual security agreement signed by the UK, US, the Benelux countries, France, Italy, Denmark, Norway, Portugal and Canada, adopted as its foundation stone the conviction that an attack on one member was an attack on all. By the end of 1950 Truman had sent four divisions to Europe, appointed Eisenhower as commander, initiated an integrated command structure and initiated plans for the rearmament of Germany.

What sort of world awaited the BAOR, to occupy in 1945 and later to defend? The air forces of the US, Russia and Great Britain had spent the last eighteen months or so systematically pounding the cities of Germany, Italy and Austria into rubble. Initially, of course, this was justified in order to dismantle the German war effort and debilitate the opposition both physically and, less successfully, psychologically. Unfortunately, though, for the British and the other occupying forces, the relentless and persistent bombing by day and by night in the last months of the war served only to maximize the rubble, the chaos and the carnage well after the job of helping to bring Germany to her knees had clearly been successfully completed. The more destruction—physical, economic and social—the more the Allies had to rebuild, refinance and reorganize, a fact not fully appreciated or accepted by the more bullish and belligerent.

Churchill saw this but did little about it in his strategy dealings with Bomber Command and with 'Bomber' Harris in particular: he accurately described post-war Europe as "a rubble heap, a charnel house, a breeding ground of pestilence and hate". Indeed, 90 percent of the buildings of Cologne, Hamburg and Düsseldorf were flattened, 70 percent of Vienna's buildings were in ruins, Warsaw was utterly devastated, 20 percent of all France's buildings were destroyed, 25 percent of Greece's; in Britain Clydebank, Hull, Coventry and London, for example, were laid waste. Across Europe the triumphant allies had to deal with some fifty million survivors of the war; sixteen million of these were termed, somewhat euphemistically, 'displaced persons', and all had to be repatriated, or resettled and rehoused. Six million Germans were displaced from Pomerania, Silesia and East Prussia to make room for the westward-moving Poles. Up to two million Germans are said to have died during these mass migrations; many of the Germans ended up in what was to become the British zone. This, of course, was ethnic-cleansing on a prodigious scale although the Allies preferred to call it 'population transfer'. The recommendation that the expulsion of the German-speaking people from Poland, Bohemia, Hungary and Rumania—about twelve million in all—and their resettlement in the overcrowded ruins of West Germany should proceed in an 'orderly and humane' fashion was somewhat reminiscent of the request of the Holy Inquisition that its victims should be put to death "as gently as possible and without bloodshed".

By the early 1950s, the Soviets had restricted emigration from within the Eastern Bloc. The Berlin Crisis of 1961 came about as the result of a loophole whereby between 1949 and mid-1961 some 2.7 million East Germans immigrated to West Germany through a gaping hole that existed between East and West Berlin. This led to a huge brain drain from East to West Germany of younger educated professionals, so that nearly 20 percent of East Germany's population had migrated to West Germany by 1961. From a Soviet point of view, something had to be done about this so that June, the Soviet Union issued a new ultimatum insisting that Berlin become a free, demilitarized city and demanding the withdrawal of Allied forces from West Berlin unless they could negotiate a deal with the Democratic Republic within the next six months allowing them to stay and permitting transit rights. This was, of course, rejected out of hand: negotiating with East Germany was tantamount to official recognition and it would do irreparable damage to Konrad Adenaur's resurgent West Germany. June 1961 saw a persistent Khruschev and the newly installed John F. Kennedy disagreeing further, leading Kennedy to ask Congress for a $3.2-billion supplement to his defence budget, the powers to call up reservists, and a further $207 million for a fallout shelter programme to protect the American people. On 13 August, East Germany erected a barbed-wire barrier that would eventually become the Berlin Wall and, outside Berlin, the Iron Curtain. The loophole was more or less closed and the haemorrhaging of intellect from east to west was staunched.

2. RECONSTRUCTION OF GERMANY

"God, I hate the Germans."

Gen Dwight D. Eisenhower in a letter to his wife Mamie, September 1944

Sentiments such as these at the highest level of allied government cannot have helped to foster an objective and broad-picture policy regarding the future of Germany within Europe.

We have seen how the Allies went on to leave much of Germany in ruins with millions displaced and millions more dead. We have also noted how, post-war, the allies split Germany, Berlin and Vienna into sectors with the US, Russia, France and Britain all getting a slice.

Early plans for the reconstruction of Germany involved de-industrialization by eradicating heavy industry and anything that could be useful in rearmament of any kind. Germany would, post-war, be a country characterized by its agrarian economy and light industry. Not a Germany anyone who knew pre-war Germany would recognize. This industrial and economic emasculation, essentially the Morgenthau Plan, was never adopted, as we shall see.

The first 'level of industry' plan was signed by the Allies on 29 March 1946; it decreed that German heavy industry was to be reduced to 50 percent of its 1938 levels by the destruction of 1,500 listed factories. In January 1946 a cap was put on German steel production, setting the maximum allowed at about 5,.8 million tons of steel per annum, that is a quarter of the pre-war production level. Britain held most of the steel plants in her occupation zone and argued for a less punitive 12 million tons of steel per year. Britain eventually gave in to the US, France, and the Soviet Union, which had urged a 3-million-ton limit. Redundant steel plants were earmarked to be dismantled. In effect Germany was to be reduced to the living standards experienced at the height of the Great Depression in 1932. Car production was limited to 10 percent of pre-war levels.

Soon after the ceasefire, the United States led the way, through Operation Paperclip, in garnering German technological and scientific expertise and intellectual property (patents and copyrights and trademarks) registered in Germany. 'Intellectual reparations' obtained from Germany have been estimated to have been worth up to $10 billion, (around $100 billion dollars in 2006). At the same time, the Allied forces began a programme of erasing Nazi influence from Germany in a process known as 'denazification"' The intellectual property and equipment taken from Germany included such items as, or plans and drawings for, electron microscopes, cosmetics, textile machinery, tape recorders, insecticides, a unique chocolate-wrapping machine, a continuous butter-making machine, a manure spreader, ice-skate grinders, paper napkin machines and "other technologies, almost all of which were either new to American industry or far superior to anything in use in the United States". Ex-Nazi scientists and engineers from major (ex-Nazi) industrial firms such as Krupp, Henkel, Farben and Flick found their way to the US and Russia (under Operation Osavakim) in particular, their way eased by the prospect of a comfortable lifestyle and excellent research and production facilities, scientific, technical and medical books and journals and instruments. The slave labour of tens of thousands, the toxic gases they had employed in concentration camps, the tanks they churned out for use against the allies were all quietly forgotten in the name of scientific progress.

To compensate for the loss of the lucrative exports generated to take the place of heavy industrial products which formed most of Germany's pre-war exports, the Germans would have to gear up their exports of coal, coke, electrical equipment,

The former Flick ironworks at Charlottenhütte. Friedrich Flick (1883–1972) was the founder of the Flick dynasty; he was found guilty at the Nuremberg trials, his industrial enterprises utilizing 48,000 forced labourers from Germany's concentration camps. (Marco Giebeler)

leather goods, beer, wines, spirits, toys, musical instruments, textiles and clothing. Timber exports too were important.

Despite these early policies, as enshrined in the Morgenthau Plan, a momentous decision was made, despite Russian and French concerns over resurgence, that Germany should be re-industrialized and rehabilitated to allow it to play a constructive role in the reconstruction of economies, societies and industries throughout Europe. This came in the 'Restatement of Policy on Germany' delivered by James F. Byrnes, the US secretary of state, in Stuttgart on 6 September 1946. This, the 'speech of hope' repudiated the Morgenthau Plan and championed a dramatic change of policy to embrace economic reconstruction, and gave Germany and the German people hope for the future. The various occupying armies, including the BAOR, would have a key role to play in overseeing, nurturing and safeguarding this massive programme of regeneration. From now on, this vision encompassed the bigger picture, viewing Germany as an integral part of European regeneration in every sense, and which would allow Germany to rearm. The new mantra was that a strong Germany would mean a strong Europe, all the better with which to oppose the Russians.

This belated realization of basic common-sense economics was one of the engines driving this volte-face. Although much of the US and British occupation costs was charged back to the Germans the money already being spent on food imports to stave off mass starvation was enormous. The radical change of policy was obviously also driven by politics and military strategy. The Western allies had been increasingly anxious that the austerity, poverty and hunger inevitable under the Morgenthau Plan would encourage the Germans to embrace communism. The policy also sent a clear message to the Soviets that the United States intended to maintain a military presence in Europe indefinitely. Ultimately, though, the new industrial policy was a shrewd move to win the hearts and minds of the German people: the prospect of prosperity, industrial and social reconstruction and rebuilding national identity under the Americans and British was far more attractive than impoverishment under the Soviets.

In July 1947, the ailing economy needed a kick-start so currency reform was initiated to check the rampant inflation. In 1948, the deutschemark replaced the virtually worthless reichsmark as the official currency of the Western occupation zones, boosting the economic recovery. The US Marshall Plan, the 'European Recovery Program' was started and between the years 1947–1952, some $13 billion of economic and technical aid—equivalent to around $140 billion in 2017—poured into to Western Europe. Despite protests the Marshall Plan, in the less generous form of loans, was in 1949 extended to also include the newly formed West Germany. Between 1949 and 1952, West Germany received loans amounting to $1.45 billion. 1949 saw the establishment of West Germany from the Western occupation zones, with the exception of the Saarland.

The economic revival was well underway with a steady rise in the standard of living, a growing export market, a reduction in unemployment, increased food production, and much reduced black market activity. During the mid-1950s, the unemployment rate in Germany was so low that it necessitated the immigration of Turkish workers and their dependents—*Gastarbeiterprogramm*—to fill job vacancies.

Government Aid and Relief in Occupied Areas (GARIOA) was a US programme in which the US from 1946 supplied emergency aid to Japan, Germany and Austria, mainly in the form of food to alleviate malnutrition and starvation. Germany benefitted from GARIOA between July 1946 and March 1950. In 1946 the US Congress had voted GARIOA funds to prevent "such disease and unrest as would endanger the forces of occupation" in occupied Germany. The funds were to be used to import food, petroleum and fertilizers. Using GARIOA to import raw materials for use in industry was *verboten*. In 1948 the combined US and UK expenditure on relief food in Germany was close to $1.5 billion. As with Marshall Plan aid, the funds received by Germany through GARIOA were charged back to the Germans. By 1953 West Germany's combined GARIOA and Marshall Plan debt was over $3.3 billion. In 1953 it was decided that West Germany was required to repay only $1.1 billion. This was repaid by 1971.

By 1950 the dismantling of heavy German industry stopped, so what was left could be brought back into service by the Germans. Equipment and plant had been removed from 706 manufacturing plants in the West and steel production capacity had been reduced by 6.7 million tons At the same time the BAOR was presiding over a country whose economy was now enjoying the benefits of the *Wirtschaftswunder*, the 'economic miracle', or 'The Miracle on the Rhine'.

The war had been won, defeated Germany had been zoned up, and the BAOR established. The ever-shifting military strategy, the economic plan and the political machinations were in place to meet the soldiers and airmen of the BAOR when they were deployed to a devastated and chaotic western and northern Germany. The job initially was to occupy Germany, keep it down and oversee its post-war life of austerity and mass hunger with its economy much reduced and suppressed and its industry emasculated. We have seen how this, of course, was all to change in response to fast-moving events, not least those engineered by Soviet Russia, but in post-war 1945 this was the situation that the BAOR found themselves in.

The big clean-up began immediately: in Berlin and in other cities the *trümmer-frauen*, the so-called 'rubble women'—many of them war-widowed or waiting the long wait for their POW husbands, brothers and sons to come home—set to work recycling bricks and slabs from the piles all around them, forming human chains, passing along buckets of salvaged bricks, knocking off the mortar and stacking them up to be reused.

German women doing their washing at a water hydrant in a Berlin street, next to the wreck of a Wehrmacht armoured car, 3 July 1945. (Sgt Wilkes, No 5 Army Film & Photographic Unit / IWM)

The Allies had issued orders requiring all women between the ages of 15 and 50 to report for this work; there was no shortage: in 1945 there were about seven million more women than men in Germany. About four million homes had been destroyed throughout Germany by Allied air raids and many factories were in ruins. Half of all school buildings were unusable and not quite half of traffic facilities rendered useless. It is estimated that these industrious women and girls processed 500 million cubic metres of rubble from Germany's wrecked towns and cities. Berlin alone accounted for about 75 million cubic metres, enough rubble to build a 600-kilometre

Rubble women in Leipzig, still at it in 1949.

wall all the way to Cologne five metres high and thirty metres thick. In cities such as Berlin, Dresden, Hamburg, Leipzig, Magdeburg or Nuremberg, special railway lines were made for the removal of debris. These 'rubble tracks' transported hundreds of millions of tons of war rubble from the centres to the outskirts of the city so that they could be buried or stacked there. Rubble women it was who loaded these tracks. Despite some recent claims that aspects of the *trümmerfrauen* have been exaggerated, they, along with thousands of prisoners of war, stand as a vivid testament to the challenges facing the Germans and their occupiers in picking up the pieces of their shattered cities.

Various organizations were set up under the auspices of the BAOR to organize and assist in the reconstruction of German cities and towns. Prominent among these were the transport units formed with German prisoners of war and called *Dienstgruppen* (DGs). Initially, they wore their German Army uniforms, but in July 1947 these were replaced by a dark-brown battledress. Later in 1947 they were redesignated to the German Civilian Labour Organization (GCLO). They had many and various uses but their main task was in supporting major BAOR exercises, using a wide range of American, ex-German army, Canadian and British army vehicles. They proved particularly valuable in the Berlin airlift: GCLO Transport Units provided the vital links between supply depots, railheads and the airfields.

In October 1950, they were reorganized again, reduced in numbers and renamed the German Service Organization (GSO). In 1957 the GSO Transport Units became Mobile Civilian Transport Groups (MCTGs). The next few years saw a significant change in role for the MCTGs. From being mainly operational transport in support of the RASC in the field, they took over running the buses for BAOR school children, family administration and the newly introduced air trooping. RCT Freight Service, which started operating in the BAOR in the late 1960s, was largely operated by MCTG vehicles and drivers.

The Corps of Royal Engineers set up works in Berlin, Schleswig, Minden, Düsseldorf, Hanover Dortmund and Hamburg, with seventeen subordinate DCRE and one independent garrison engineer for the Hook of Holland. They controlled fourteen German artisan groups and three plant groups. These groups were organized on military lines and consisted mostly of ex-servicemen who were dressed in green battledress. The initial works centred on the redeployment of the British forces, and the majority of the commitment was met by the rehabilitation of German barrack. Many diverse enterprises were undertaken, a typical example being the provision in Hamburg of office and storage accommodation for twenty consulates and fifty sponsored industrial firms. The Berlin airlift brought additional tasks including work on airfields in the British zone and arrangements to fly in coal. Other work carried out included building roads, temporary camps and store sheds, laying railway track, providing light for shift working and a variety of ancillary tasks which were mostly undertaken by employing directly enlisted labour.

One of the largest items in the redeployment plan was the construction of the Hohne Barracks at Lüneburg Heath where accommodation to be provided included four officers' and sergeants' messes, four other ranks' cookhouses, fifteen office blocks and 200 married quarters; in addition there were to be four NAAFI canteens, workshops, garages, sports grounds, schools, cinemas and the necessary churches. Access to the field firing area had to be provided for tanks by construction of two miles of concrete road. Provision of married quarters was a continually increasing commitment. By the middle of 1950 some 1,100 quarters had been provided by the German authorities under RE supervision and 250 quarters were actually under construction but many more were still required. At this time the Germans were persuaded to embark upon a new project known as Operation Build. This operation was to provide married quarters planned and built by the Germans themselves on the understanding that if and when they were not required for British families they would be de-requisitioned and handed over to the local German authorities.

The Mixed Service Organization (MSO) was a civilian arm of the BAOR made up of displaced citizens of eastern European nations occupied post-war by the Soviets. They did invaluable support work as drivers, clerks, mechanics and guards. They were originally formed as watchman and labour units in the immediate aftermath of the war and were made up of former POWs, concentration camp inmates and forced labourers (slaves). The MSO was organized in a structure similar to British colonial units, with a British commanding officer and senior non-commissioned officers overseeing a 'native' officer and NCO structure. The Transport Service was disbanded in the late 1980s. Members of the MSO were known as 'Mojos' by British servicemen.

German civilians cooking an impromptu meal on the street at the end of the war. (Bert Hardy, No 5 Army Film & Photographic Unit / IWM)

The MSO was divided into several specialist services: MSO Armed Guard Service, guarding army installations; they wore navy blue battledress uniforms and were armed with obsolete .303 calibre Lee-Enfield rifles; MSO Dog Handlers, guarding army installations; MSO Labour Service, providing manual labour, controlled by the Royal Pioneer Corps and MSO Transport Service, driving four- and ten-ton lorries, coaches and tank transporters, controlled by the Royal Army Service Corps then the Royal Corps of Transport.

At the end of the war, there were over two million displaced Poles in Europe, the remnants of the fourth largest Allied army, behind the USSR, the US and Great Britain. After the war, with all the consternation regarding Poland's future and its eventual incorporation into the Soviet Bloc many Poles faced a future in exile with no independent homeland to return to. Some remained in Germany and were absorbed into military guard companies within BAOR.

In 1947 the first British units employing Poles were established at Fallingbostel on the site of the POW camps, the very camps in which some of the Poles had been imprisoned. 317 Unit MSO RASC was the first Polish tank transporter unit taking Diamond Ts and other equipment from 15 Company RASC. In 1952, 312 Unit MSO RASC, the second Polish Tank Transporter Unit, was formed. These two units were based at Fallingbostel and Hamm.

3. GARRISONS, BARRACKS, TRANSPORT & TRAINING

Prior to World War II, the small British army was essentially used to expand, protect and garrison the British empire, a force devoted to keeping what was pink on the world map pink. Only war necessitated the British army's presence on the European continent in any meaningful capacity, as evidenced by the world wars in 1914 and 1945. In 1918 the British army eventually left Europe and was largely demobilized. In 1945 this did not happen. As we have seen, the BAOR was formed on 25 August 1945 with the eventual stationing of 77,000 or so men on the North German Plain, along with their families. BAOR was disbanded in 1994 but even then it took a further twenty-five years before British troops finally pulled out.

The 77,000—and the numerous ancillary and support staff these troops required—had to be organized and garrisoned, they had to be barracked, they had to be transported expediently and efficiently as required, and they had to be trained to the highest possible specification at the highest state of readiness. All of these factors were essential if the BAOR was to operate as a credible and forceful deterrent to the Warsaw Pact forces they faced; all were vital if the BAOR was to delay any invasion by the Warsaw Pact.

Life on exercise: detachment commanders' course, Roermond. (David Chrystal)

Covering fire. (David Chrystal)

40 Signal Regiment HQ and staff, Sennelager. (David Chrystal)

Garrisons

The regiments of the BAOR were allocated to three garrisons.

Bergen-Hohne Garrison

Bergen-Hohne Garrison was a major garrison with facilities located close to Bergen at Lager Hohne, at Lager Oerbke near Fallingbostel and at Celle in Lower Saxony. It was home to the 7th Armoured Brigade and most of its support units. Two separate brigades occupied the bases during the Cold War that later became Bergen-Hohne Garrison: the brigades were Fallingbostel, Wolfenbüttel and Celle; its headquarters, 207th Signal Squadron and an ordnance company were based in Soltau. Hohne housed the 22nd Armoured Brigade. Both brigades were part of the 1st Armoured Division, which also included the 12th Armoured Brigade (headquartered at Osnabrück) and had its divisional headquarters and signals regiment at Verden on the River Aller. Four to 5,000 British soldiers were stationed in the garrison until its closure in 2015. The Bergen-Hohne Training Area was part of the garrison. The garrison population with families and civilians varied between 10,000 and 12,000.

Westfalen Garrison

Westfalen Garrison was formed out of the former garrisons at Paderborn and Gütersloh; it has facilities located in Paderborn, Sennelager and Gütersloh and currently forms the major part of British Forces Germany. Due to close in 2019, it is the home of 20th Armoured Brigade and most of its subordinate units. Headquarters for Westfalen Garrison is based at Antwerp Barracks, Sennelager. The oldest part of Paderborn Garrison is Neuhaus at Paderborn, dating back to 1370 and which became Horrocks Barracks after the war. The main part of Paderborn Garrison has its origins in the Infantrie Kaserne, which was built in the early 20th century on Elsenerstrasse, and the Panzer Kaserne, which was built in the 1930s on Driburgerstrasse, and that went on, after the war, to become Alanbrooke Barracks and Barker Barracks respectively. Linsingen Kaserne, later Gordon Barracks, was built in Hamelin in the 1930s. At Herford, Estorff Kaserne and Stobbe Kaserne were built in 1934: after the war these became Hammersmith Barracks and Wentworth Barracks respectively. Also at Herford, Otto Weddigen Kaserne was built around the same time to become Harewood Barracks. More barracks were established at Sennelager. Gütersloh Garrison came out of two RAF stations: RAF Sundern which was handed over by the RAF to the British army as Mansergh Barracks in 1961 and RAF Gütersloh which was handed over as Princess Royal Barracks in 1993. The present garrison was created as part of the Ministry of Defence's Army Basing Programme when Paderborn and Gütersloh garrison merged to form the new 'super-garrison', Westfalen Garrison, on 1 April 2014. Hameln Station was handed back in November 2014 and Herford Station was handed

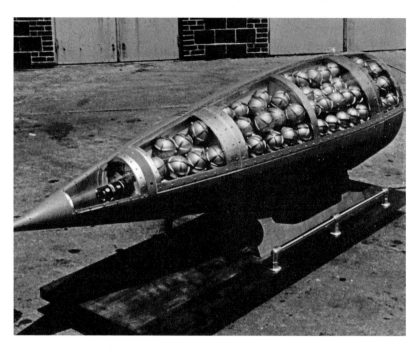

A M190 Honest John chemical warhead section containing demonstration M134 GB (Sarin) bomblets. c. 1960. (Historic American Engineering Record, LoC)

back, once 1st Armoured Division had changed role and then moved to York, in June 2015. Facilities under the garrison's control include the Sennelager Training Area.

Osnabrück Garrison
Facilities located at Osnabrück in Lower Saxony and Münster in North Rhine-Westphalia. It was home to the 4th Armoured Brigade and most of its subordinate units. Am Limberg Kaserne was built during the war in Osnabrück as an ammunition factory for the Wehrmacht; this was expanded in the early 1950s to become Imphal Barracks (for cavalry and tank regiments) and Mercer Barracks (for infantry regiments); it is now being redeveloped for housing. The site on Landwehrstraße once was Quebec Barracks. The garrison was once the largest British military base outside the UK. It closed in 2009.

Barracks
Many BAOR regiments took over former Wehrmacht barracks or *kasernen*. Many were built between 1935 and 1936 to satisfy the demand created by Germany's militarization and the need to accommodate a rapidly expanding number of troops and increasing amounts of matériel. One of the things that immediately strikes even the casual observer is the symmetry integral to the construction of many of these

barracks. Those accommodating troops (*mannschafts barracke*) typically comprised a square formed with the end block usually being a headquarters or utility block (*werkschafts barracke*) housing the cookhouse. A good example is Northampton Barracks at Wolfenbüttel. The parade ground would usually be in the middle of the square. The other noticeable thing about some of the *kasernen* is their architectural beauty, as with Hobart Barracks, Detmold and Paderborn's Horrocks Barracks. The 1935/6 barrack construction programme also helped ease unemployment: somebody had to build them.

The wonderful and superbly researched website www.baor-locations.org/aboutus gives us some fascinating barracks detail, redolent of true German efficiency: "For the *Mannschafts Barracke* blocks the living area tended to be on three floors. The floors would be split in two halves with two sections in each. The troops would then share communal rooms with the section commander having a single bunk. There would also be an attic and cellar. The cellars would be used not only for storage, but also as shelters (*luftschutz* bunker) for when the allies strafed or bombed the camps. Examples of this can still be found on the walls at Mansergh Barracks, Guterslöh, where the words '*Zu Schutzraum*' are still visible. To reduce the chance of injury, screens were built externally from brick around the windows offering limited light, but protection from shell splinters ... On entering the attic another bunker would be found. These were used by the fire sentries to give advance warning—should the building start to burn. The sentry was also expected to fight fires, removing the incendiaries that crashed through roofs and into attics before a blaze could take hold. Also in the attic, vast amounts of sand would be laid evenly throughout the entire floor space, extinguishing the fire once it had raged enough for the ceiling to collapse.

The quality of the accommodation is also seldom appreciated: the windows were double glazed, beach floors, marble window sills and solid oak banister rails. These privileges were not only limited to the officers' mess. It came as standard. Another quality was the size of the corridors ... These were after all designed for a Thousand Year Reich." For the officers quartered on camp, accommodation would be prefixed appropriately to that rank of officer. Many of the quarters in Fallingbostel and Hohne are still designated so to this day and can be identified by the following: L: Leutnant/ Lieutenant; H: Hauptmann/ Captain; S: Stabsoffizier/ Staff Officers (Oberstleutnant/ Lieutenant Colonel and above); G: General; BG: General Staff.

Transport

Not that many BAOR servicemen know about the former YMCA Windmill, the only British canteen on a German autobahn; it lasted from 1946 to 1971 and was situated near Beckum on the A2 Raststätte Vellern, direction Hanover–Berlin. During that time many servicemen stopped for a cup of tea and a snack here while convoys stopped here for a break.

By 1948/9 most military traffic took the Harwich–Hook route using the troopships SS *Vienna*, SS *Empire Parkestone* and SS *Empire Wansbeck*. A special troop train left Liverpool Street Station to connect with the overnight sailing to the Hook; there was also an early morning departure from Parkestone Quay. From the Hook there were three, later two, dedicated troop trains daily to serve the BAOR garrisons. One took the mainline direct to the Dutch–German border at Bentheim then travelled via Osnabrück–Bremen–Soltau, finally terminating in Hamburg. The second went via Emmerich–Dalheim, the Ruhr–Hamm–Bielefeld–Hanover again terminating in Hamburg. In the

Berlin in 1946, (Schwarz / Bundesarchiv)

late 1940s there was also an express service via Osnabrück to the then HQ BAOR/RAF(G) in the Bad Oeynhausen–Buckeburg area and a more convenient connection with the then overnight Berlin sleeper. With the reorganization of the BAOR into I British Corps area, air trooping from Luton (subsequently Stansted) to the airheads at Düsseldorf, Gütersloh, Hanover Wildenrath and Berlin was more economical and rail movement ended in the early 1960s apart from the Berliner. Until 1955 there was an additional daily troop train to and from the Hook to Klagenfurt for British Troops Austria.

Training
Bergen-Hohne Training Area
Bergen-Hohne Training Area (NATO-Truppenübungsplatz Bergen or Schießplatz Bergen-Hohne) is now a NATO military training area on the southern part of the Lüneburg Heath, covering 284 square kilometres making it the largest military training area in Germany.

It was established by the Wehrmacht in 1935 and was requisitioned at the end of World War II by the British. It subsequently played a major role in training BAOR troops during and after the Cold War. As we shall see, part of it was used as a camp for survivors of the Bergen-Belsen concentration camp, which was on the edge of the training area close to the town of Bergen. It was a key BAOR base during the Cold War, very much on the front line, forming part of 1st Armoured Division and the home to the 7th Armoured Brigade (Desert Rats) from 1947. Up to 50,000 British, American and German soldiers were stationed there at one time.

British control has seen the training area much expanded and, since the 1960s, it has also been used by the German armed forces (Bundeswehr) and other NATO troops.

Troops have trained here from as early as the 19th century, when the army of the Kingdom of Hanover drilled here. The first plans for the military training area saw the light of day in August 1934 as part of the military re-armament of the German Reich. Some 3,635 inhabitants in twenty-five villages had to leave their homes. Around a hundred barrack blocks, fifty stables and forty large garage blocks were built, as well as a hospital, storage depots and a target factory, where targets for the firing ranges were made at the eastern perimeter of the area, near the village of Belsen, and called in those days the Ostlager or East Camp. To the south of this camp was a military ammunition dump for infantry munitions. On 4 May 1936 the first units moved in.

On 15 April 1945 the training area was taken over by the BAOR, initially only making use of the eastern part of the area as a Royal Armoured Corps training centre.

The British army burning Belsen to avoid further contagion.

Right: Margot and Anne Frank's grave at Bergen-Belsen, Germany. (Arne List)

Below: A POW camp for German women outside Brussels that held Heer, SS, Luftwaffe and civilian women. (Lt O'Brien, No 5 Army Film & Photographic Unit / IWM)

During the Cold War the area was intensively used by troops garrisoned on the North German Plain. In 1957 the Bundeswehr was permitted to use the training area; on 1 April 1958 the British army transferred the training area to the Bundeswehr. Up to 50,000 British, American and German soldiers were stationed at Bergen-Hohne and it became the largest military training area in Europe and one of the key training areas for NATO's ground forces in the Federal Republic of Germany.

Troops from Germany, Netherlands, Britain and Belgium still use Hohn,e regularly putting to the test equipment including Challenger 2 and Leopard 2 tanks, Apache helicopters and artillery on the numerous ranges. Troops can also practise urban warfare and deep-wading skills there, while the area has been used increasingly in recent years by unmanned aerial vehicles, with it being the only training area in Germany where it is permitted to fly reconnaissance drones.

Münster Training Area & Münsterlager

Truppenübungsplatz Münster is a military training area in Germany on the Lüneburg Heath comprising two separate areas: Münster North (Münster-Nord) and Münster South (Münster-Süd). The two areas are separated by the town of Münster and several barracks. When the military training area was established a camp or *lager* was built about 1.5 kilometres from the town centre which became known as Münsterlager.

In 1916 Breloh Camp was built in north Münster by a regiment of gas warfare engineers (Gaspionier-Regiment'). In January 1917 the Prussian war office issued an order for the construction of a facility for gas munitions. Three factories were erected for the manufacture of chemical warfare material and associated munitions. Production began in July that year and, by the end of the First World War, extensive facilities had been built, most of which were operational. During World War II an extensive range of tests was carried out on a frighteningly wide variety of shells of various calibres, as well as on mines, projectiles,

Belgian POWS at Münsterlager, 1914.

bombs (up to 500kg) and spray equipment. The substances tested included arsenic oil, hydrogen cyanide, mustard gas (Lost), tabun, sarin, cyanogen chloride, phenacyl chloride, Adamsite, Aeroform, Excelsior (10-chlor-9,10-dihydroacridarsin) and many more.

When the site was occupied by British forces in 1945 the chemical installations were demolished and most of the stocks of chemicals were destroyed. In spite of that, Gasplatz Breloh has left behind a lethal legacy which remains one of the largest areas of residual contamination caused by armaments in Germany. Since April 1956 there has been intensive work to clear the pollution.

After the occupation of the site by British forces in 1945 the British Occupying Power established the largest POW release camp in Germany. In Münster and Breloh about 1.7 million POWs were admitted and returned home. At the facility at Hornheide, Breloh refugee camp was set up. In 1956 Münster was the base for important military instal-lations for the Bundeswehr. Around the same time the Training Area Headquarters, the Garrison Staff, the Armoured Vehicle Training Centre (formerly the Armoured Forces School), the 9th Armoured Demonstration Brigade (Panzerlehrbrigade 9) with the Panzergrenadier School, the Armoured Demonstration Battalion and the Panzergrenadier Demonstration Battalion, 53 Trials Unit (Erprobungsstelle 53) (today the Chemical Defence Research Establishment (Wehrwissenschaftliches Institut für Schutztechnologien, or ABC-Schutz) and other units and organizations were established.

Sennelager Training Area & Camp

Sennelager Training Area (Truppenübungsplatz Senne) near Paderborn covers an area of 116 square kilometres. The name Sennelager translates as 'camp on the Senne', a name originating in 1851 when the Prussian cavalry used the area as a

Sennelager ranges.

Above left: Panbashing on exercise.

Above right: Wherever the army goes, the padre goes too.

Below: The arrival at Cuxhaven of the troopship HMT *Halliday*. Families of British servicemen disembark. (S/Sgt Bentley, No 5 Army Film & Photographic Unit / IWM

training camp. It later expanded into a full training facility for the armed forces, most notably during the reign (1888–1918) of Wilhelm II. At the end of World War II in 1945, the base passed briefly to the United States Army, before its handover to the British.

The area contains several British settlements, and businesses have sprung up there to cater for this market, including a 'traditional' British corner shop (Little England), several tax-free car dealerships and some British pubs as well as a NAAFI supermarket and electrical goods dealer (SSVC). In a skit on old Carlsberg beer advertisements from the 1980s, British soldiers used the phrase "Sennelager: probably the worst lager in the world" when referring to the training area.

NBC (nuclear, biological, chemical) suits are designed to provide protection against direct contact with and contamination by radioactive, biological or chemical substances and some types of radiation, they can protect the user for up to several days. Now known as the CBRN suit. (David Chrystal)

An abandoned tank at Sennelager. The troops appear to be undertaking some sort of casualty evacuation training. (David Chrystal)

Above left: Detachment commanders' course. Roermond. (David Chrystal)

Above right: Banks of radio relay equipment. (David Chrystal)

The Soltau-Lüneburg Training Area (SLTA)

The Soltau-Lüneburg Training Area (SLTA) on the Lüneburg Heath was a British and Canadian military training area in the north of the British zone from 1963 to 1994. It came about by the Soltau-Lüneburg Agreement between the Federal Republic of Germany, the United Kingdom and Canada. The agreement allowed troops to conduct exercises the year round with the (not unreasonable) proviso that villages and farms were not to be used as military objectives and armoured vehicles could not move on Sundays or public holidays.

Around 1,800 landowners were obliged under the agreement to make their property available to the military. As a result of the constant traffic of armoured vehicles training, the heathland of the red areas soon became a wasteland. Areas were not out of bounds like the usual military training areas and there were cases of accidents resulting from civilians handling munitions. During the 1970s, an average of 1,500 armoured vehicles and 30,000 soldiers exercised in the training area each year under the terms of the agreement.

Constant training and exercises were a routine and regular feature of the BAOR. One of the most extensive and successful exercises was Operation Lionheart held in 1984. Troops were deployed in the exercise area combat zone in Hohne, Lower Saxony. Lionheart did not follow a pre-planned schedule. The main events were determined in large part by actions and reactions of individual unit commanders. All the normal phases of battle were rehearsed, including a covering force battle, a main defensive battle, river crossings, counter-penetrations and counter-attacks.

It involved 131,565 UK personnel, regular, reserve and TA, the largest exercise since the end of the war. Two hundred and ninety flights from the UK transported 32,000 personnel. This initial air movement was followed by 150 sailings across the North Sea and English Channel using civilian ferries. The sea routes carried 23,600 personnel with 14,000 vehicles and trailers. A total of 750 main battle tanks were involved and most crossings over the Rhine were conducted with combat bridging, making the assumption that all civilian bridges had been destroyed. I (BR) Corps was deployed with the 3th and 4th armoured divisions and 1st Infantry Division.

Providing the opposition (Orange forces) were 6,300 German (1 Panzergrenadier Brigade), 3,500 Dutch (41st Armoured Brigade), 3,400 American (1st Armoured Brigade) and 165 Commonwealth (from Australia, New Zealand and Canada) personnel. Lionheart was the first time US forces had operated in Europe with their new M1 Abrams MBT and M2 Bradley combat vehicles. The newly reformed 5th Airborne Brigade also formed a second opposition group, joined by elements of the Life Guards and 10th Gurkha Rifles.

Exercises continue to this day, well past the BAOR era. Here 1st Battalion Princess of Wales's Royal Regiment Warrior infantry fighting vehicles are being refuelled from an Oshkosh wheeled tanker during NATO Exercise Allied Spirit 8, January/February 2018. (MoD)

Some 13,000 RAF personnel were involved, deploying Harrier and the newly introduced Tornado aircraft.It was the first opportunity to conduct a major exercise with Challenger 1 main battle tanks, Saxon and tracked Rapier. Though still in early development, the Warrior mechanized infantry combat vehicle was also introduced. Three soldiers died during the exercise and seven were seriously injured.

British families arrive in Germany. (S/Sgt Bentley, No 5 Army Film & Photographic Unit / IWM

4. THE IRON CURTAIN & THE BERLIN WALL

"Hard as bourgeois politicians and writers may strive to conceal the truth of the achievements of the Soviet order and Soviet culture, hard as they may strive to erect an iron curtain to keep the truth about the Soviet Union from penetrating abroad, hard as they may strive to belittle the genuine growth and scope of Soviet culture, all their efforts are foredoomed to failure."

Andrei Zhdanov, Stalin's chief propagandist, used the term against the West in an August 1946 speech

The Iron Curtain went up 12 September 1944 and the Berlin Wall came down in 1991. The Inner German Border (IGB), *die Grenze*, or Iron Curtain was the demarcation line which sliced Germany in two and which kept the Germans in the German Democratic Republic (East Germany) apart from their compatriots in the Federal Republic (West Germany). It was conceived on 12 September 1944 in London when the United States, the Soviet Union and Great Britain agreed on the track of the demarcation line between the future zones of occupation of the Western Allies and the Soviet Union. This, of course, subsequently dictated the line of the old border between the Federal Republic of Germany and the German Democratic Republic. The line was established regardless of geographical, historical and economic considerations and without any expression of the free will of the German people.

The length of the border between the Federal Republic of Germany and the GDR amounted to 1,393 kilometres. It was interspersed with extensive barrier systems and other devices intended to prevent citizens of the German Democratic Republic from crossing into the Federal Republic of Germany. In 1983 these barrier systems included 1,283 kilometres of mesh fencing, 45 kilometres of double barbed-wire fencing, 154 kilometres of antipersonnel minefield or some 3,000 mines per kilometre, 385 kilometres of automatic firing devices (SM70 totalling 37,200 explosive charges), 795 kilometres of vehicle hazards (ditches and dragons teeth), 1,283 kilometres of six-metre-wide ploughed and harrowed strip, and vehicle track, 148 kilometres of arc lamps in front of villages, 1,393 kilometres of border communications system, 721 prefabricated pillboxes, 134 earthen bunkers, 721 concrete observation towers, 60 command posts attached to observation towers 84 kilometres dog runs, 250 dog runs with some 1,029 dogs, 1,160 kilometres hinterland security fence and 16 kilometres of walls in front of villages. To make it less appealing the wall also featured a wide area known as the 'death strip' that contained anti-vehicle trenches, fakir beds and other off-putting defences.

The Iron Curtain.

Between 13 August 1961—the date when the Berlin Wall came up and the blocking of the border intensified—and 1983 a total of 172 people died attempting to escape. Despite this situation citizens of the GDR repeatedly succeeded in escaping to the Federal Republic of Germany. The average between 1974 and 1983 was twenty-eight a year. The IGB manifested in rural areas by double fences made of steel mesh with sharp edges, while around urban areas high concrete barriers similar to the Berlin Wall were built. The erection of the Berlin Wall in 1961 more or less ended a dec-ade during which the divided capital of divided Germany was one of the easiest places to navigate west across the Iron Curtain. In 1952 Stalin advised the East Germans to build up their border defences, telling them, "The demarcation line between East and West Germany should be considered a border—and not just any border, but a dangerous one ... The Germans will guard the line of defence with their lives." The border between the western and eastern sectors of Berlin, however, remained open. Berlin then became a magnet for East Germans desperate to escape life in the GDR, and also a flashpoint between the United States and the Soviet Union.

Separate international economic and military alliances prevailed on each side of the Iron Curtain: member countries of the Council for Mutual Economic Assistance and the Warsaw Pact, with

What's left of the 'iron curtain' at Devínska Nová Ves, Bratislava, Slovakia. (Vladimír Tóth)

the Soviet Union as the leading state, and member countries of the North Atlantic Treaty Organization (NATO) and with the United States as the pre-eminent power.

The Iron Curtain, then, was a potent symbol of the BAOR's role in Germany, with BAOR troops patrolling it thus reassuring West Germans that they were being defended against Warsaw Pact invasion. Rhine army reconnaissance troops constantly patrolled the border where it fell in the British sector, accompanied by an officer of the British Frontier Service—veritable experts on every yard of the Curtain—and by West German border guards, all flying the flag for the West and checking for any changes to the demarcation line. Behind the menacing towers with their armed and all-seeing guards were the propaganda rooms from which intermittent broadcasts boomed out within earshot of neighbouring West German towns and villages lauding the good life in the East and decrying the miserable existence in the West.

If ever a soldier or airman stationed in West Germany as part of the BAOR needed reminding why he or she was there, then they only had to look east; eventually the forbidding Iron Curtain would loom into sight. Likewise, anyone stationed in the British sector of Berlin pondering their existence would be similarly reminded by the grimmest of barriers, the Berlin Wall. The Berlin Wall was always as much a profound ideological and political symbol as it was a physical barrier.

Above: American soldiers at Checkpoint Charlie, December 1961; note the anti-tank bazooka. (Berliner Mauerarchiv)

Left: This bus was going nowhere after a failed May 1963 escape attempt. (Polizeihistorische Sammlung des Polizeipräsidenten von Berlin)

The Border Brigade of the East German riot police use mirrors to make it difficult for photographers in the west to take pictures of residents along the Berlin border being forcibly removed from their homes, October 1961. (Horst Siegemann, Archives of the Land of Berlin)

An elderly woman standing at the Berlin Wall in the western sector has waited three hours to see her relatives in East Berlin, shortly after the wall went up. (Dan Budnik / Library of Congress)

To the GDR authorities the Berlin Wall was the Anti-Fascist Protection Rampart (*Antifaschistischer Schutzwall*); to West Berliners it was the 'Wall of Shame', a term acidly coined by mayor Willy Brandt. Before the Wall went up, some 3.5 million East Germans had defected from the GDR, many by crossing the border from East Berlin into West Berlin whence they could travel to West Germany and to other Western European countries. Notwithstanding, after the Wall went up, over 100,000 people attempted to escape of whom over 5,000 people succeeded. Estimates of the death toll range from 136 to more than 200 in and around Berlin.

If a BAOR soldier wanted to go on holiday to West Berlin and take in a trip to the Soviet sector, then he had a number of options. Four autobahns connected West Berlin to West Germany, the most famous being the Berlin–Helmstedt autobahn, which

Leaving West Berlin at the Brandeburg Gate.

Above and below: Berlin Wall showdown with Soviet tanks facing off against US tanks for sixteen hours, 27/28 October 1961.

British Ferret armoured car on the road to Spandau. The British closed the road on 13 August 1961. (Horst Siegemann, Archives of the Land of Berlin)

entered East German territory between Helmstedt and Marienborn (Checkpoint Alpha), and which entered West Berlin at Dreilinden (Checkpoint Bravo for the Allied forces) in southwestern Berlin. Access to West Berlin was also possible by four rail routes, the most popular being from Braunschweig. Once in West Berlin passage to the East would be through Friedrichstraße station in East Berlin or, more likely, through Checkpoint Charlie. Berlin itself was never a part of BAOR; after the war it remained a 'city under occupation' as agreed at Yalta and Potsdam. Comfortable and enjoyable as it was for the troops stationed in the British sector, it remained a symbol of isolation, cut off from the West by miles of East Germany. Getting from West Berlin to West Germany was a heavily monitored process with Warsaw Pact troops watching travellers at every stage, be they on military duty or BAOR personnel on holiday. Trains were patrolled by menacing-looking armed East German guards; the few road links permitted no stopping except in an emergency while ninety minutes were allowed for the transit from East to West and vice versa with every west-bound or West Berlin-bound vehicle checked at the checkpoints. Should a vehicle not arrive within the ninety minutes then the East German guards were mobilized to come looking. Air corridors were the only other way in or out.

5. NUCLEAR & COMBAT READINESS

To reiterate, with the formation of the NATO unified command structure in 1951, BAOR became an integral part, along with Belgian, Canadian, and Dutch army units, of the Northern Army Group (NORTHAG). BAOR was a crucial feature of NATO's panoply of ground forces to deter or, if deterrence failed, to repel a major Warsaw Pact offensive on northern Europe. To facilitate this and maximize its combat effectiveness, from the early 1960s, BAOR was equipped with tactical nuclear weapons, the first formation of the British army trained to engage on a nuclear battlefield. The deployment of a nuclear-ready BAOR was a tangible and visible demonstration of British defence policy relating to European security and was the military means by which Britain was intent on deterring a conventional or nuclear Warsaw Pact attack.

To quote David French: "By the late 1960s BAOR had developed a twin-track war fighting doctrine. On the one hand it showed how tactical nuclear weapons could be employed from the outset of a crisis. But on the other hand, it showed how BAOR

It was avoiding this that gave BAOR its *raison d'être*. This is nuclear weapon test Mike at Enewetak Atoll, the first hydrogen bomb ever tested, on 1 November 1952. (National Nuclear Security Administration Nevada)

might conduct a prolonged period of operations using conventional weapons to buy time for NATO's political leaders to negotiate a peaceful end to a crisis without resort to the use of nuclear weapons. But if BAOR was to mount either kind of operation it needed sufficient soldiers to do so, they required modern and effective weapons, equipment and stores, and they had to be adequately trained to use them."

We can add to this the fact that BAOR's potential use of nuclear weapons was also designed to prevent the BAOR being completely overrun by Warsaw Pact forces. Manoeuvres that it conducted between 1949 and 1952 suggest, through BAOR, the British army's readiness and expectation to fight in Europe, the decisive theatre.

MGR-1 Honest John Short Range Tactical Battlefield Support Missile System

The MGR-1 Honest John rocket was the first nuclear-capable surface-to-surface rocket in the United States arsenal, first tested 29 June 1951 with the first production rounds delivered January 1953. The first Army units received their rockets by year's end and Honest John battalions were deployed in Europe in early 1954. Before launch they were assembled in the field, mounted on an M289 launcher and aimed and fired in about five minutes by a team of six men.

The two basic versions of Honest John were MGR-1A (M31) with a maximum range of 15.4 miles, and an improved version, the MGR-1B, entered service in 1960; this system was phased out with the introduction of the MGM-52 Lance system. The missile flew at speeds of Mach 1.5 and was unguided, powered by solid propellant; the warheads were either a 680kg (1,500lb) high explosive (HE) or a 5/25-kiloton nuclear warhead. Its launch vehicle was normally a truck-based transporter, erector, launcher (TEL). A single rocket was carried on a long launch rail. Two types of truck-mounted launchers were used, both based on the M139 5-ton truck. This gave the Honest John a reasonable off-road capability and good mobility on roads. Length: 7.57m (24ft 10 in), weight: 2136kg (4,710lb), minimum range: 7.2km (4.5 miles), maximum range: 37km (23miles)

By 1961 24 Missile Regiment had assumed a nuclear role with Honest John at Barker Barracks in Paderborn. Two other regiments shared this deployment: 50 Missile Regiment at Northumberland Barracks in Menden and 39 Missile Regiment at Dempsey Barracks in Sennelager, from 1960. All three were also equipped with M115 8-inch nuclear capability howitzers. The Honest John was unguided so wind was a factor in any launch: each launch was allocated a wind measurement trailer.

Despite it all and the chilling *raison d'être* for their existence in BAOR Germany, it is unlikely that many troops or their dependents spent that much time agonizing over their potentially precarious location. Nevertheless, a swift scan through *The British Army of the Rhine NBC Guide* would have made disturbing reading when it was published in October 1981. The threat of coming under a nuclear, biological or chemical (NBC) attack launched from behind the Iron Curtain remained a real very possibility. NATO military forces would have been the target of course but weapons of mass destruction (WMD) are notoriously indiscriminate and it would only take a slight change in wind direction to implicate civilians within the target zone, including BAOR families. And it was not just NBC hardware coming from the east—BAOR ordnance was just as capricious when it came to wind speed and direction—the possibilities for a hostile attack on Warsaw Pact forces to the east quickly turning into friendly fire were enormous.

That revised leaflet would have brought the situation home with its compelling detail, relating crucial information and instructions in the event of an outbreak of nuclear or chemical warfare. As regards the latter, nerve and blister agents are described, along with how to manage your respirators, how to detect a chemical agent, and, in the event of an attack, the required immediate action procedures, first aid and decontamination drill. Also there are the different German civil and British military siren-note warnings; the advice given for sounding a chemical alarm, by contrast, is to "Bang together metal objects, or repeated bursts on vehicle horns."

There is detail regarding the various types of nuclear explosions (airburst, surface burst, underground) and effects (bright flash, immediate radiation, heat, blast, residual radiation, fallout), along with the immediate action drill required, protection from the residual hazard and decontamination procedures, as well as the medical effects of a nuclear attack.

In January 1963 the tactical nuclear weapons available to the British Army in Germany were 8-inch howitzers, Honest John rockets and Corporal guided weapons in numbers generally in line with those available to other NATO members.

The Soviets continued to maintain their near monopoly of chemical weapons in Europe, the operational implications of which were extremely serious for NATO forces since they had no offensive capability in this area. Worst of all, though, was that Soviet ground forces in Eastern Europe had recently received new tactical ballistic nuclear missiles of improved accuracy, the SS21 and SS22, both of which represented a significant threat to the rear areas of British ground forces. In the case of the SS22, that threat extended back to the Channel ports.

By 1984, the Warsaw Pact forces could boast 18,000 tanks on the central front. Countering a prodigious armoured thrust continued to be the number one priority of I British Corps; to that end both main battle tanks were improved: the new thermal

The Minister of State for the Armed Forces, Mr. John Stanley, reported that the new Challenger tank had started operational service in BAOR, and Challenger regiments were increased to five. Tracked Rapier and the first Saxon wheeled armoured personnel carriers had also started operational service. The first MCV80 tracked APCs started trials with the infantry, and the first field trials of Ptarmigan, the secure trunk communication system, had also begun. The equipping of all front-line Lynx helicopters with the TOW anti-tank missile was completed. The reorganization of 1st British Corps was completed, giving the corps stronger reserves, as well as two additional armoured regiments by the end of the year. The trials of 6 Brigade of 1st British Corps in an air mobile role had begun.

The bad news is that the inexorable strengthening of Soviet and Warsaw pact ground forces in eastern Europe and in the western military districts of the Soviet Union continue apace. Soviet main battle tank production is still at around 3,000 tanks a year, and the latest Soviet tank, the T80, is coming into service in East Germany. The last 12 months have seen continued expansion of the already massive Warsaw pact holdings of conventional and nuclear artillery in eastern Europe and increased numbers of armoured personnel carriers and Hind attack helicopters. Just as significant are the dramatic improvements in the ability of the Soviet ground forces facing NATO to sustain intensive operations on the central front using supplies and equipment pre-stocked in eastern Europe, and in East Germany in particular, thus reducing dependence on long supply lines back to the Soviet Union itself. The Warsaw pact's stockpiles of ammunition, fuel and tactical pipeline-laying equipment in eastern Europe mean that it could sustain operations against NATO for some 60 to 90 days, twice as long as was the case only five years ago in 1979.

House of Commons debate, 22 October 1984

imaging sight for both Chieftain and Challenger was in production, an integral component of new tanks but also retrofitted to Challenger and Chieftain tanks already in service. Improvements were made to Challenger's and Chieftain's fire control systems which were further improved with a new 120mm high-pressure gun and new ammunition.

Anti-armour missile capabilities were improved and the need for an effective, man-portable high-penetration weapon was addressed. The infantry in Germany was progressively equipped with the light anti-armour weapon, LAW 80, a massive improvement on the Carl Gustav 84mm man-portable reusable anti-tank recoilless rifle. The Milan anti-tank missile was in service throughout I British Corps and issued

The Russian Mil Mi-24 (Миль Ми-24); NATO reporting name: Hind) is a large helicopter gunship, attack helicopter and low-capacity troop transport with room for eight passengers. It has been operating since 1972 by the Soviet Air Force and its successors, along with more than thirty other nations. The Hind has been called the world's only 'assault helicopter' due to its combination of firepower and troop-carrying capability. (Igor Dvurekov)

to nearly all reinforcing infantry battalions, including TA battalions: no less than half of the I British Corps' mobilized strength.

Other improvements included Swingfire, the long-range tracked vehicle-mounted anti-tank missile fitted with a thermal imaging sight and an improved warhead. Similar improvements were provided for Milan, and an improved warhead for TOW, the helicopter-borne anti-tank missile also in service. Research and development work was underway for the next generation of anti-tank missiles to replace Milan, Swingfire and TOW in the 1990s in partnership with France and Germany.

As for the infantry, more protected mobility and faster vehicles were provided by Saxon just coming into service and MCV 80 which was being trialled. The existing SLR was replaced with the SA80 rifle and machine gun both using the new NATO 5.56mm ammunition. The SA80 rifle now had a telescopic sight, together with a complementary night sight. It also enjoyed an automatic-fire capability, which the SLR did not have. It was lighter, thus allowing more ammunition to be carried.

As if the 80,000 tanks massed against the BAOR were not enough there was also more than 8,000 Warsaw Pact artillery pieces on the central front, many of which were capable of firing nuclear and chemical shells as well as conventional ammunition. A dire need for better artillery with better crew protection was identified: two new artillery improvements for I British Corps were the multi-launched rocket system, to replace the 175mm M107 gun, and the SP 70, to replace the 105mm Abbot. Both came into service around the end of the 1980s. There were further improvements to target-acquisition capability through the use of remotely piloted vehicles, and to battlefield surveillance through the use of airborne radars in manned aircraft. By the end of the 1980s I British Corps had very greatly improved artillery support in terms of firepower, range, accuracy and survivability.

It should, of course, not be forgotten that I British Corps had to contend with a major threat from the air which largely came from increasingly sophisticated Soviet fixed-wing aircraft with a ground-attack role, and perhaps most dangerously of all from Soviet ground-attack helicopters such as the Hip and the Hind, the deployment of which on the central front had doubled since 1980.

Tracked Rapier was already in service in 1984, thereby greatly improving the mobility and survivability of air defence. The Rapier system was itself improved, and, by the end of 1984 all towed Rapier units had increased immunity to electronic counter-measures and improved radar. That same year, Javelin, the development of Blowpipe, also came into service and greatly enhanced the lethality of that air-defence missile system.

Ptarmigan, the secure communications system, came into operational service with I British Corps in 1985, as did Wavell, a sophisticated data-processing system for brigade commanders and above. Bates, the computer based artillery targeting system, came into service toward the end of the 1980s. Ptarmigan, Wavell and Bates each substantially improved I British Corps' C 3—consultation, command and control—capability.

The BAOR arguably achieved its highest state of efficiency, potential effectiveness, preparedness for the apocalypse, and readiness in the mid-1980s. But this operational apogee was by no means always the case. From as early as the late 1940s the Rhine army was vulnerable, undermanned and under-resourced, to say the very least. The parlous situation is catalogued in a series of official statements issued by the Foreign Office in various COS committee reports; we learn of the potentially precarious position of BAOR

> To show the relative importance of the BAOR, in 1984 the British army comprised 50,000 troops on the Rhine, about 9,000 in Hong Kong, about 2,500 in the Falklands, about 3,000 in Cyprus, some in the Sinai, perhaps 2,500 in Gibraltar and a few more in Belize. The direct public expenditure cost of the Rhine army was about £2.6 billion in 1984.

A Soviet T-64 of the 21st Motor Rifle Division in Perleberg in the 1980s. (Ashot Pogosyants)

Field training in Germany, discretion sometimes being the better part of valour. (Courtesy of Catherine Holt PWRR & Queen's Museum)

George Cook in an FV432 armoured communications vehicle on what looks like a Family Day. The FV432 is the APC variant of the FV430 series of armoured fighting vehicles. Since its introduction in the 1960s, it has been the most common variant, being used for transporting infantry on the battlefield. In the 1980s, almost 2,500 vehicles were in use, with around 1,500 still in operation today, mostly in supporting arms. (Courtesy of George Cook)

due its dependence on German labour for administrative support: the 150,000 Germans working for the BAOR could be rendered unreliable due, for example, to communist infiltration: "our forces there would ultimately be greatly handicapped and movement on any substantial scale would be difficult." Furthermore, in the Royal Signals "the present strengths [...] would make the provision of adequate communications forward of

Germany: postwar occupation zones.

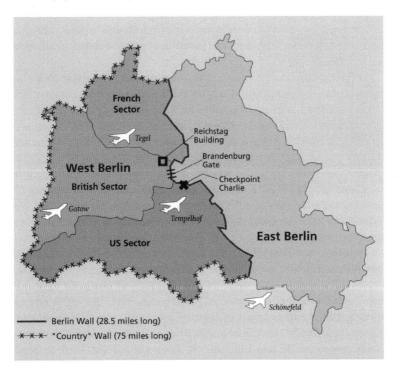

Berlin: occupation zones and the Wall.

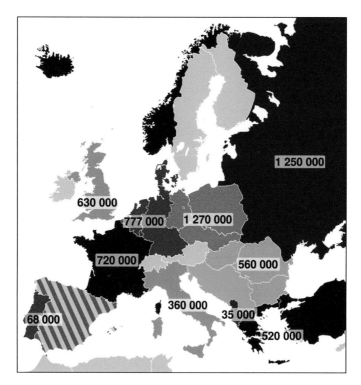

Europe 1959 NATO and Warsaw Pact troop strengths

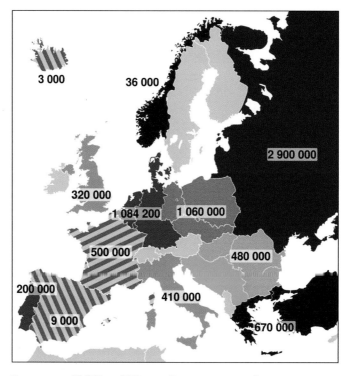

Europe 1973 NATO and Warsaw Pact troop strengths

Cultural treasures awaited troops and their families in Paderborn, like this one, the Town Hall, when they explored 'beyond the wire', which many did in increasing numbers as the years went by. The author lived here 1964–69. (ludger1961)

Schloß Neuhaus (Paderborn) von der Gartenfront aus gesehen, the 1370 Paderborn Castle, which became Horrocks Barracks post-1945. (Nawi112)

Barker Barracks, Paderborn, pre-1945 the Panzerkaserne (Tank Barracks) Paderborn. Currently it is home to the 20th Armoured Infantry Brigade. The author's father was stationed here 1964–69 as a WOII with the 24th Missile Regiment, RA. (MoD)

Tank range 7 B with control tower near Ostenholz at the Bergen-Hohne training area, Germany. (Hajotthu)

East Berlin Death Strip as seen from the Axel Springer Building, 1984. The author looked out of the same window days after the wall came down while on a business trip to Axel Springer Verlag/Ullstein AG. (George Garrigues)

Old Iron Curtain near Cizov, CZ, 25 October 2009. (Cuchulainn)

A German Leopard tank in Sennelager mud on driver's instruction course. (David Chrystal)

Harrier jump jet undergoing service. (David Chrystal)

English Electric Lightning (XN776), a supersonic jet fighter, at the National Museum of Flight in East Fortune, East Lothian, Scotland. It is displayed in the colours of 92 Squadron, based at RAF Gütersloh, where it served until 1977. The author recalls that the very first thing he saw of West Germany when he landed at RAF Gütersloh in September 1964 was a row of Lightnings. (Ad Meskens)

Zafari and Harry with their handlers from 102 Military Working Dogs Squadron taking part in a live fire exercise at Sennelager. (MoD)

A Challenger 2 main battle tank with The Queen's Royal Hussars (QRH) during a live firing exercise at Hohne, Germany. The tank entered service in 1998, successor to the BAOR'S Centurion. (MoD)

Queen's Royal Hussars (The Queen's Own and Royal Irish) (QRH) Junior Non-Commissioned Officer (JNCO) Cadre course at Sennelager. (MoD)

Above: An FV432 armoured personnel carrier at Sennelager. (David Chrystal)

Below: The T-64 is a Soviet second-generation main battle tank introduced in the early 1960s. This is a T-64B or Ob'yekt 447A (1976). (Сергій Попсуєвич)

Above: Fourteen years after the end of the BAOR a parachutist of the SPAG (Submarine Parachute Assistance Group) jumps from an RAF C-130 Hercules during Exercise Bold Monarch in 2008. During the two-week exercise, three submarines, one each from the Netherlands, Norway and Poland, were bottomed to simulate sinking. Support personnel and equipment from Canada, France Germany, Greece, Israel, Italy, Netherlands, Norway, Poland, The Russian Federation, Turkey, Ukraine, United Kingdom and United States worked together to solve complex rescue and medical problems in a variety of demanding scenarios. The exercise marked the first time that Russia participated in such an exercise and was a significant step forward in the development of a truly international rescue capability.

Left: A NAAFI poster from a 1950s Christmas.

Headquarters Northern Army Group very difficult." Rear of Headquarters Northern Army Group the situation was "deplorable. Even if existing units are made up to Higher Establishment, the barest essential communications cannot be provided". The position of the infantry varied considerably by battalion but all battalions were short of men and support companies had been "pared to the bone". The Royal Air Force was equally vulnerable because in the event of an emergency the army could not take over stocks of aviation fuel stored in Antwerp and deliver it to RAF airfields unless more trained personnel were available. The RAF was "at the moment in danger of a breakdown in the command organisation due to deficiencies of Signals personnel" as well as having its operations seriously curtailed due to shortages of personnel and resources. The chiefs of staff demanded as essential that reinforcements were "trained men, in every way qualified and fit to undertake the operational tasks required of them".

In the event of a Soviet attack, the outlook was positively bleak: the British were anxious to assure the Germans that the Allies would hold the river Elbe in case of a Soviet push, but there was no sign of a Plan B other than to fall back to the Rhine. The effect on the army of manpower shortages during the withdrawal phase following a Soviet attack was alarming: "the delay imposed on the Russians will be reduced as the covering forces as at present constituted will be too weak. ... The danger of successful airborne *coup de main* action against both the Rhine and Maas bridges will be greatly increased. During the initial phase of the Rhine battle, the inability of all arms and services to deploy a reasonable fighting potential will cause unacceptable delay in the preparation of the Rhine position."

The much-feared invasion of West Germany and the Low Countries, of course, never materialized and we can only speculate on the course it might have taken and on the possible consequences. It might, however, be instructive to look at the 1979 Warsaw Pact 'Seven Days to the River Rhine' military simulation exercise to get an idea of what might have happened to the BAOR. 'Seven Days' adumbrated the Soviet bloc's vision of an apocalyptic seven-day nuclear war between NATO and Warsaw Pact forces. The classified World War III scenario was released by the Polish government in 2005, with a view to "draw a line under the country's Communist past" and "educate the Polish public about the old regime".

The *casus belli* was that NATO launched a nuclear strike on Polish cities in the Vistula river valley, a first-strike scenario, and on Czech cities, to prevent Warsaw Pact commanders from reinforcing East Germany in a bid to stem a projected NATO invasion of Poland. Two million Polish civilians were expected to perish and all Polish military forces would be extirpated. Polish operational strength would be completely destroyed. A Soviet nuclear counter-strike would then be launched against West Germany, Belgium, the Netherlands and Denmark, implicating the BAOR.

East Germans commemorate the 25th anniversary of the Berlin Wall, 13 August 1986, with a parade by Kampfgruppen zum Mauerb. (Klause Franke / Bundesarchiv)

The Group of Soviet Forces in Germany would form the vanguard of the Warsaw Pact invasion; the GSFG comprised five armies, each with three or four tank and motor-rifle mechanized infantry divisions. In the North, the force would consist of the Soviet Second Guards Tank Army, Twentieth Guards Army and Third Shock Army, comprising seven tank divisions and five motor-rifle divisions. East Germany's National People's Army, the cream of the non-Soviet pact forces, would contribute two tank and four mechanized-infantry divisions. Operational manoeuvre groups using elements of, or whole tank armies, would then be deployed to exploit the breakthrough: following hard on the heels of the motor-rifle units, heavily supported by artillery, helicopters and close air support aircraft would have broken the BAOR/ NATO front. An operational manoeuvre group might include two tank divisions and three to five motor-rifle divisions.

The Guardian finishes it off: "A series of red mushroom clouds over western Europe show that Soviet nuclear weapons strikes would have been launched at Germany, the Netherlands, Denmark and Belgium if Nato had struck first. Red clouds are drawn over the then German capital, Bonn, and other key German cities such as the financial centre of Frankfurt, Cologne, Stuttgart, Munich and the strategically important northern port of Hamburg. Brussels, the political headquarters of Nato, is also targeted ... The exercise indicated Warsaw Pact forces aimed to reach the Franco-German border within a week of a Nato attack."

6. ROYAL AIR FORCE & ROYAL NAVY

The RAF

Air cover and support for BAOR was provided by what was Royal Air Force Germany (RAFG), a command of the Royal Air Force and part of British Forces Germany. It comprised units in Germany, initially established as part of the occupation after World War II, and later as a key contingent of the RAF's commitment to the defence of Europe during the Cold War. The commander of RAFG doubled as commander of NATO's Second Allied Tactical Air Force.

Second Allied Tactical Air Force (2ATAF) was a NATO military formation under Allied Air Forces Central Europe whose task it was to provide air support to NATO's NORTHAG. 2ATAF commanded all flying units based within its sector and all reinforcements flying into its sector, as well as ground-based radar systems and stations, air defence units and the airfields in its sector.

It was formed in 1958 with a responsibility covering the Netherlands, Belgium, and Germany north of Kassel and south of the river Elbe. Commander of Second Allied Tactical Air Force was the commanding air chief marshal of the British RAF Second Tactical Air Force, which was renamed RAF Germany on 1 January 1959.

Headquarters of 2ATAF were at RAF Rheindahlen; in the event of war the command centre for 2ATAF and NORTHAG was at Joint Operations Center Maastricht (JOC Maastricht) in the Netherlands. In 1983 NATO began the construction of Static War Headquarters Castlegate at Linnich, Germany, to replace JOC Maastricht. Alternate War HQ was located at Kanne in Belgium north of Fort Eben-Emael. Second Allied Tactical Air Force commanded the British Royal Air Force Germany, the Belgian Air Force, the Royal Netherlands Air Force, two divisions of the German Air Force (the Luftwaffe) and one US Air Force tactical fighter group, as well as extensive air defence and radar installations provided by Germany, Belgium and the Netherlands.

If required 2ATAF would have been reinforced with units from the US Third (UK-based), Eighth (reconnaissance and bombing), Ninth (immediate reinforcements) and Twelfth (follow-on reinforcements) air forces and with French Air Force and RAF units. At the start of hostilities 2ATAF would immediately have had around 700 combat aircraft on hand.

2ATAF was disbanded on 30 June 1993 and replaced by Allied Air Forces Central Europe.

Before 2ATAF, from 1954 69, 102, 103, 104, 149 squadrons, and later 59 Squadron at RAF Gütersloh were equipped with Canberra bombers. This force was under

Bomber Command control from Britain and had been moved to Germany because of overcrowding of suitable airfields in the UK. With the establishment of the British nuclear bomber forces in the context of NATO's strategy of massive retaliation the Canberra bomber squadrons were withdrawn from Germany.

After 1955, most of the air bases were handed over to the newly established German Air Force and RAF Bückeburg to the army of the German Armed Forces. The number of RAF squadrons was reduced both because of NATO's nuclear strategy and for financial reasons after the Suez fiasco. By 1959 2ATAF was focused on six main bases: RAF Bruggen, RAF Geilenkirchen, RAF Gütersloh, RAF Jever (No. 2 Squadron, flying Swifts), RAF Laarbruch and RAF Wildenrath. The key aircraft were the Canberra night-fighting fighter-bomber working from three stations and the Hunter day fighter stationed at two stations. From 1960, there two stations were on alert around the clock. Canberras loaded with tactical nuclear weapons could be ready in fifteen minutes. Available also were Swifts used as scouts and four squadrons of Gloster Javelins as all-weather interceptors. Two English Electric Lightning squadrons—92 Squadron RAF and 19 Squadron RAF—arrived in Germany as of 1964. Jever was transferred in 1961 and Geilenkirchen closed in 1968: 3 Squadron RAF moved to Laarbruch and 92 Squadron RAF moved to Gütersloh, reducing the command to four flying airfields. RAF Germany was disbanded as a separate command in 1993 as part of the reduction of British Armed Forces presence in Europe at the end of the Cold War. The remaining RAF forces in Germany became 2 Group RAF, part of RAF Strike Command; 2 Group was itself disbanded on 1 April 1996 when it was absorbed into 1 Group RAF.

The flying units of 1989 were as follows:

RAF Rheindahlen
doubled as commander of NATO;s Second Allied Tactical Air Force

4 Wing, administrative control of RAF Regiment Rapier squadrons based in West Germany

33 Wing, administrative control of RAF Regiment light armour squadrons based in West Germany

RAF Bruggen, FRG
No. 9 Squadron, 12 x Tornado*
No. 14 Squadron, 12 x Tornado*
No. 17 Squadron, 12 x Tornado*
No. 31 Squadron, 12 x Tornado*
No. 37 Squadron RAF Regiment, (air defence, 8 x Rapier launch stations)
No. 51 Squadron RAF Regiment, (light armour, 15 x Spartan, 6 x Scorpion)
(* with nuclear strike capability with 18 x WE.177 tactical nuclear weapons)

RAF Gütersloh, FRG

No. 3 Squadron, 16 x Harrier
No. 4 Squadron, 16 x Harrier
No. 18 Squadron, 16 x CH-47 Chinook (supporting BAOR)
No. 230 Squadron, 16 x Puma HC.1 (supporting BAOR)
No. 63 Squadron RAF Regiment, (air defence, 8 x Rapier launch stations)

The station was built around 1935 and active in 1944/5 with Ju 88 nightfighters of 5./NJG 2 (Nachtjagdgeschwader 2) as part of the Defence of the Reich defensive aerial campaign. The Americans took the station in April 1945 and was designated as 'Advanced Landing Ground Y-99', laying down a 4,000-foot SMT hardened runway The Ninth Air Force operated F-4 Lightning and F-5 Mustang reconnaissance aircraft of the 363rd Tactical Reconnaissance Group in late April. The P-38 Lightning-equipped 370th Fighter Group operated from Gütersloh until the German surrender on 8 May 1945. The 370th remained until the airfield was handed over to the RAF as part of the formation of the British Occupation Zone of Germany on 27 June 1945, as Headquarters No. 2 Group RAF.

From 1958 RAF Gütersloh came under the operational command of 2ATAF, as with all other RAFG stations. The RAF initially built a 1,830-metre-long runway, which was later extended to 2,252 metres. It was home to two squadrons of the English Electric Lightning F2/F2A: 92 Squadron RAF and 19 Squadron RAF from 1968 to 1976. These provided two aircraft for the quick response alert, able to scramble within minutes. It then became home to 3 Squadron RAF and 4 Squadron RAF which flew variants of the BAE Harrier. With the departure of the Harriers, the RAF continued to operate helicopters from here: 18 Squadron RAF with the Boeing Chinook and 230 Squadron RAF with the Puma HC1. RAF Gütersloh closed and was transferred to the British Army on 30 June 1993 to become Princess Royal Barracks, a base for British Army helicopters, and Royal Logistic Corps regiments.

RAF Laarbruch, FRG

No. 2 Squadron, 12 Tornado GR.1A (reconnaissance)
No. 4 Squadron, Harriers
No. 15 Squadron, 12 x Tornado*
No. 16 Squadron, 12 x Tornado*
No. 20 Squadron, 12 x Tornado *
No. 1 Squadron RAF Regiment, (light armour, 15 x Spartan, 6 x Scorpion)
No. 26 Squadron RAF Regiment, (air defence, 8 x Rapier launch stations)
(* with nuclear strike capability with 18 x WE.177 tactical nuclear weapons)

Left: A 4 Squadron pilot plots his mission: 4 Squadron RAF flew the BAE Harrier GR.7 version from 1992 until the unit was relocated to RAF Cottesmore in 1999. (David Chrystal)

Below: Engineers from 4 Squadron pose in front of FO Godfrey's Harrier at RAF Laarbruch. (David Chrystal)

RAF Wildenrath, FRG

No. 19 Squadron, 16 x Phantom

No. 92 Squadron, 16 x Phantom

No. 60 Squadron, Andover CC.2 transport planes

No. 16 Squadron RAF Regiment, (air defence, 8 x Rapier launch stations)

The Royal Navy

When World War II ended, the Royal Navy, in one guise or another, played a vital role in the BAOR dealing with the turmoil following the cessation of hostilities in the British zone of occupation. Though vital, most of the naval establishments were short-lived and had closed by the end of 1946, Wilhemshaven by the end of 1947. Royal Navy activity in Cuxhaven, Hamburg and Kiel ended in the mid-1950s while HMS *Royal Prince* at Krefeld closed in the early 1960s. In Operation Eclipse—the British plan for the situation straight after the German surrender and the creation of the British zone of occupation—the plans for the navy included processing the surrender of all German naval vessels, the disarming and dispersal of all naval personnel, the identification and clearance of all maritime minefields and, most importantly, the destruction of any facility that might give Germany any opportunity to challenge the supremacy of the Royal Navy in European waters.

RN assets and their post-war duties included: HMS *Princess Irene* shore location was the Royal Navy Headquarters in Berlin in 1945. HMS *Princess Louise* was based in Brunsbuttel, at the mouth of the River Elbe from 1945 to 1946. Responsibility was for the clearance of German naval minefields in the Elbe estuary and the entrance to the Kiel Canal. The degaussing of ships was also carried out here: that is neutralizing the magnetic field of a ship by encircling it with a conductor carrying electric currents.

Cuxhaven was home to HMS *Augusta*, the administrating unit for RN minesweeping activities in German home waters from 1945 to 1946. HMS *Royal Albert* 1946–1954: this shore establishment was based at the former German Kriegsmarine base at Cuxhaven; likewise from 1946–1948 under the Allies, the 2nd Division of the German Minesweeping Administration, responsible for the clearing of mine fields off the German coast in the North Sea; HMS *Royal Charlotte*, a naval intelligence unit, from the autumn of 1945, after moving from Kiel.

The Aquatic Warfare Training Unit for BAOR was in the Eckernförde area in 1949. Captain C. H. Petrie RN was responsible for the commissioning of a German hospital ship (*KMB 8*) in the harbour as HMS *Royal Prince* in Emden 1945/6. It was also responsible for the operation of port facilities, disarming of ships and sailors, and the control of captured/surrendered personnel. HMS *Royal Prince* later moved to Krefeld from 1949 to 1960.

HMS *Royal Edgar* was in Hamburg from 1945 to 1947 looking after port administration. RN/RM Elbe Flotilla/ Squadron operated out of Hamburg too from 1945 to 1958 and was responsible for the safe passage of all BAOR waterborne traffic from the border with the Soviet zone east of Buchen and the Elbe estuary. The unit was equipped with fast patrol boats, including some former wartime Kriegsmarine vessels, crewed by both Royal Navy and Royal Marine personnel. The unit was renamed Elbe Squadron in the mid-1950s before being disbanded in 1958 when its responsibilities were handed over to the newly created Bundeswehr.

117 Infantry Brigade Royal Marines (May–July 1945) including the 31st, 32nd and 33rd battalions RM was posted from England to Kiel in mid-May 1945 in order to release the 46th Highland Brigade for duties elsewhere in Schleswig-Holstein. Duties included provision of a guard force for all naval installations in the city, the disarming and initial screening of all German naval personnel and subsequent dispersal to concentration areas in line with Operation Eclipse, also processing the arrival, by sea, of civilian refugees from the Soviet-occupied areas of Eastern Germany including East Prussia. The brigade left Kiel in July to return to the UK and disbandment.

The Baltic Fishery Protection Service was a covert naval intelligence unit operating in the Baltic under Royal Navy command in ex-Kriegsmarine fast patrol boats manned by ex-Kriegsmarine personnel. The task was subsequently taken over by the newly formed Bundesmarine in 1955.

HMS *Royal Prince* was based in Krefeld from 1947 to 1960, after moving from Emden. Rhine Flotilla/ Squadron 1958 was based on HMS *Royal Prince* in 1958 at Krefeld, responsible for the safe passage of all waterborne traffic along the Rhine between the Dutch border and the French Zone south of Bonn. The unit was also required to maintain military expertise in the planning and execution of major river crossings in the event of any projected attack by Soviet or Warsaw Pact forces. The unit was equipped with fast patrol boats and a number of landing craft crewed by both Royal Navy and Royal Marine personnel. The unit was renamed Rhine Squadron in the mid-1950s before being disbanded in 1958 when its responsibilities were transferred to the Bundeswehr.

Royal Marines Demolition Unit/ Special Boat Section Royal Marines based at HMS *Royal Prince* in Krefeld in the late 1940s/ early 1950s was the unit tasked with contingency planning for the close protection and demolition if and where required of the key strategic bridges over the Rhine in the event of an attack by Soviet forces based in East Germany.

1 Commando Brigade Royal Marines (including 45 and 46 commandos) was one of the first British units to enter Lübeck in early May 1945. After the final surrender of Germany the brigade handed over control of the city (except for the docks) to the 15th Scottish Division, and deployed north along the Baltic Coast as a guard force, as well

The arrival at Cuxhaven of the troopship HMT *Halliday*. Families of British servicemen disembark. (S/Sgt Bentley, No 5 Army Film & Photographic Unit / IWM)

as carrying out security duties in the Travemunde docks (the river Trave formed the boundary between the embryonic British and Russian zones of occupation in this area). The brigade returned to the UK in July 1945.

HMS *Royal Henry* was stationed in Minden from 1945 to 1946, and served as the Headquarters Allied Naval Command Expeditionary Force (HQ ANCXF).

4 Commando Brigade Royal Marines (including 47 and 48 commandos) was redeployed to Minden from the Dutch coast immediately after the German surrender to provide the guard force for HQ ANCXF and associated occupation duties in the neighbouring area. The Brigade returned to the UK (via Warburg) in late 1945 and was disbanded in early 1946.

HMS *Royal Alfred* in Plön was Headquarters Flag Officer Schleswig-Holstein between 1945 and 1946, responsible for the overall command of the many RN establishments operating throughout Schleswig-Holstein and the western Baltic waters. The site of a Kreigsmarine training establishment, it was initially occupied by 6th Guards Tank Brigade and then handed over to the Royal Navy who remained there for about a year. In 1946, it was handed back to the army and renamed Connaught Barracks.

7. INTERNATIONAL SUPPORT

Canada

The BAOR was reinforced in their role on an ongoing and ever-present basis by Canadian Forces Europe (CFE) during the Cold War. CFE comprised two formations in West Germany, Canadian Forces Base Lahr, with the 4th Canadian Mechanized Brigade Group (1957–1993), and No. 1 Air Division RCAF at Canadian Forces Base Baden-Soellingen, which later became 1st Canadian Air Group. Both formations closed in the early 1990s with the end of the Cold War.

Canada's presence in Europe as part of NATO forces began in 1951, when the 27th Canadian Infantry Brigade Group (CIBG) was deployed to Hanover attached to the BAOR. This formation moved to a permanent base at Soest in 1953. Initially, the strategy was to rotate brigades to Germany: the 27th CIBG was replaced by 1st CIBG in October 1953, in turn replaced by 2nd CIBG in 1955, and then 4th CIBG in 1957. Before the arrival of 4th CIBG each brigade had only been equipped with a squadron of main battle tanks; with 4th CIBG this was strengthened to a full armoured regiment equipped with Centurions and an independent brigade reconnaissance squadron with Ferrets. In 1959, when 4th CIBG's tour was due to end, it was decided to keep it and its associated brigade units in place. The brigade headquarters were at Soest. Individual units were stationed both at Soest and other towns in North Rhine-Westphalia: at Soest BHQ one infantry battalion, service units; at Hemer one infantry battalion, one artillery regiment; at Werl one infantry battalion, one engineer regiment, field ambulance; at Iserlohn an armoured regiment.

1953 to 1971 saw a large garrison of Canadian soldiers and their families at Soest with the camps located just east of the town in Bad Sassendorf as well as at Werl and Hemer-Iserlohn and Deilinghofen to the southwest. (There were also several Belgian *kasernes* located in Soest. In addition, there was an American Nike missile battery (66th Battalion) situated to the south, which was subsequently turned over to the German military.)

From 1971 to 1993, the former Canadian properties, including the married quarters along Hiddingser Weg, south of the B-1, were used and occupied by the British military personnel and their families. The former CLFEX (the Canadian army's food and clothing store for NATO families) was converted to a NAAFI under the British and finally demolished in 2006.

In 1962, there were further reinforcements when the brigade was bolstered with the addition of the Royal Canadian Armoured Corps helicopter recce troop, equipped with nine CH-112 Nomad helicopters and CH-136 Kiowa helicopters, later to be known as 444 Squadron RCAF. By the middle of the decade the 4th CIBG could boast 6,700 troops in three mechanized infantry battalions, a reconnaissance squadron equipped with both armoured vehicles and helicopters, artillery equipped with both fire support and tactical nuclear weapons, and an extensive logistic operation. It was rebadged the 4th Canadian Mechanized Brigade Group in May 1968.

The Canadians not only offered invaluable ground support. No. 1 Air Division RCAF was posted to Europe in the early 1950s with four Royal Canadian Air Force bases in France and West Germany. These included RCAF Station Marville (No. 1 Wing) and RCAF Station Grostenquin (No. 2 Wing) in France and Royal Canadian Air Force Station Zweibrücken (No. 3 Wing) and Royal Canadian Air Force Station Baden-Soellingen (No. 4 Wing) in West Germany. Each wing comprised three fighter squadrons. Eight squadrons were replaced by nuclear strike aircraft in 1962 in Canada's new nuclear strike role.

In 1963, the French government announced that all nuclear weapons on French soil, NATO or French, would now be controlled by France. This was unacceptable to the RCAF and other NATO units stationed in France, so the two nuclear strike squadrons at 2 Wing were moved in 1963: 430 Squadron to 3 Wing Zweibrücken, and 421 Squadron to 4 Wing Baden-Soellingen. Remaining non-nuclear armed units in France were relocated to Marville, and RCAF Station Grostenquin.

Scene from the Royal Signals Detachment Commanders' course at Sennelager. (David Chrystal)

Captain David Chrystal coming out of the 13 Signal Regiment mess tent at Sennelager, unimpressed with his bacon sandwich. (David Chrystal)

40 Signals Regiment on exercise at Sennelager. (David Chrystal)

Grostenquin was closed in 1964 and its units transferred to RCAF Station Marville which itself closed in 1967 when France withdrew from NATO; the units transferred to the new RCAF Station at Lahr (later CFB Lahr, then the civilian Flughafen Lahr). RCAF Station Zweibrücken was closed in 1969.

Army units stationed at CFB Lahr were organized under the 4th Canadian Mechanized Brigade Group and were mostly heavy armour Cold War tank formations using Centurion tanks then the Leopard 1 or mechanized infantry equipped with the M113 family of armoured personnel carriers.

Belgium

In preparation for Operation Overlord, the Belgian army, the Brigade Piron, comprised three infantry heavy all-arms mobile columns. After the German surrender the brigade moved to the Münster area as part of the British zone of occupation tasked with disarming former German soldiers, collecting and guarding all abandoned military equipment and re-establishing essential civilian services. Brigade headquarters was established in Oelde, with infantry battalion headquarters at Sendenhorst, Ludinghausen and Wadersloh. Regimental HQ of their artillery regiment was also at Ludinghausen. In December 1945 the brigade returned to Belgium for disbandment. Following the establishment of NATO and NORTHAG, Belgium committed an army division. Its tactical area of responsibility was the southern edge of the former British zone with elements of a brigade permanently based around Soest—complementing the Canadian NATO brigade—and elements of a second brigade in the Troisdorf area to the east of the Rhine near Cologne.

Denmark

After Germany's capitulation the new Danish government wasted no time in re-establishing its infrastructure and raising a new army. The Danes agreed to provide a brigade-sized reinforcement for the British occupation zone of Germany for an initial period of two years; this deployed in March 1947 and consisted of three infantry battalions, an artillery regiment with other supporting arms and basic logistic infrastructure. Initially the Danish Brigade deployed to Friesland in the very northwest of the British zone replacing the departed Canadian Army of Occupation and disbanded Free Polish Division.

After NATO was set up Schleswig-Holstein was handed over to the Danish and Norwegian brigades and most British army units left the area. In autumn 1949 the Danish Brigade moved from Friesland to Itzehoe to the north of Hamburg, reducing to 1,200 men and then increasing again to 1,800. The British 5 Army Group Royal Artillery (5AGRA) with its headquarters in Oldenburg replaced the Danish units in Friesland.

A new defence plan for the Jutland peninsular involved a defence based on the Kiel Canal with the Danes taking the west, and the Norwegians the central and eastern sectors. The British Armoured Car Regiment remained in NeuMünster. The formation became known as the South Jutland Land Covering Force. The Norwegian Brigade was redeployed to the north of Norway in autumn 1953, the Danes remained in Itzehoe until 1958 when Germany assumed responsibility for the defence of Schleswig-Holstein.

Malta

The Royal Malta Artillery (RMA) was part of the British army, used as a missile transport wing for the British and US armies. The 1st Regiment, Royal Malta Artillery first arrived in BAOR in 1960, posted to Moore Barracks, Dortmund and then on to Wrexham Barracks, Mülheim, where they served until 1978.

Norway

The plan was that each of the twelve Norwegian brigades would spend six months in Germany. The advance party of the first Norwegian contingent (Brigade 471) arrived in Cuxhaven on 13 January 1947 with 4,200 personnel in total. Brigade 522 was the last Norwegian contingent to serve in Germany, between October 1952 and April 1953.

Poland

When the war ended, elements of the valiant 1st Polish Armoured Division and equally valiant 1st Polish Independent Parachute Brigade found themselves in the far northwestern corner of Germany. Here they were to remain until 1947 when the Soviets installed a communist government in Poland. The units were disbanded although some of the troops remained in Germany and joined the newly formed paramilitary MSO which created units such as the 617 Tank Transporter Company. Other roles included guards, dog handlers, labourers, and many more.

The Netherlands

Following the establishment of NATO, in 1950 the Dutch government agreed to make a military contribution to the defence of Western Europe which included the permanent stationing of a brigade group in northern Germany. The brigade headquarters and key units were established in Seedorf, a small village near Zeven, between Hamburg and Bremen. Other major units were stationed in the Hohne area. The brigade was initially known as 121st Light Brigade but subsequently was rebadged 41st Mechanized Brigade. There was also a Dutch garrison in Blomberg, north of Paderborn and to the east of Detmold.

8. DENAZIFICATION & FRATERNIZATION

As if the BAOR did not have enough to contend with straight after World War II, what with tens of thousands of displaced refugees pouring into their zone and Soviet hordes massing just over the border, there were also the two vexed questions of de-Nazification (*Entnazifizierung*) and fraternization: to fraternize or not to fraternize with the Germans.

Denazification was a well-intentioned but impractical Allied initiative to cleanse pre-war and wartime German and Austrian society, culture, press, economy, judiciary, and politics of any vestiges of Nazism. This was to be achieved by removing from

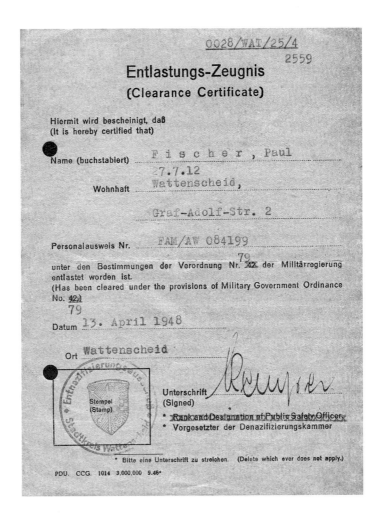

Paul Fischer's *entlastungszeugnis* (clearance certificate) 0028/WAT/25/4 2559, effectively a 'denazification' document.

positions of power and influence those who had been Nazi Party members and by disbanding or emasculating the organizations associated with Nazism.

About 8.5 million Germans, or 10 percent of the population, had been members of the Nazi Party. Nazi-related organizations added enormously to this number, for example, the German Labour Front (25 million members), the National Socialists People's Welfare Organization (17 million), the League of German Women, Hitler Youth, the Doctors' League, and others. It was the Nazi Party and these organizations that were the engines driving the Nazi state, implicating up to 45 million Germans. Some 90 percent of German lawyers had been members of the Nazi Party. By early 1947, the Allies held 90,000 Nazis in detention; another 1.9 million were permitted to work only as manual labourers. The problems surrounded effective denazification were many and various—and impossibly huge.

However, things looked promising when in April 1945, as American troops advanced on Munich, Hanns Huber a German anti-Nazi salvaged from imminent official pulping and oblivion a nearly complete list, with photographs, of Nazi Party members compiled since its foundation. This amounted to fifty tons of vital information; now it became possible to verify claims about participation or non-participation in the party. Incredibly at first the Americans showed no interest, so Huber started to put the files into some order. It was only when a civilian American archivist, who by chance happened to be in the vicinity, realized what they were actually sitting on did things start to move forward that November. The 1.5 million Germans who had joined the party before Hitler came to power were immediately deemed to be hard-core Nazis. But the list, to some extent, was a poisoned chalice.

The necessary bureaucracy required that a *fragebögen* form, a questionnaire, be completed by anyone suspected of implication in Nazism. Progress was agonizingly slow in processing the forms: up to 40,000 forms might arrive in a single day requiring attention. By December 1945, even though a full 500,000 forms had been processed, there was a backlog of four million from POWs and civil camps and a potential case load of seven million. By June 1946 66,000 Germans had been arrested and were languishing in civil internment camps. Five hundred went to trial and two years after VE Day two million *fragebögen* had been processed with 350,000 Germans excluded from office. The *fragebögen* were, of course, completed in German but the number of Americans working on denazification was totally inadequate. To make matters worse, by 1947 American troops were expecting to be completely withdrawn from Europe.

There was now pressure to find Germans deemed suitable to run their own country. Exacerbation of the dire situation came in January 1946 in a directive from the Control Council entitled 'Removal from Office and from Positions of Responsibility of Nazis and Persons Hostile to Allied Purposes' announcing, among other things, exclusion from public office and/or restriction to manual labour as one the punishments for involvement in Nazism. At the end of 1945, 3.5 million former Nazis still awaited classification, many of them barred from working in the meantime. By the winter of 1945/6, 42 percent of public officials had been dismissed. To add to the problems, malnutrition was widespread, while the economy demanded fit and active supervisors and workers to clear away debris, rebuild infrastructure, to earn foreign exchange to buy food and other essential resources.

Blunders, negligence and over-zealous behaviour were rife, as exemplified by Paul Kistermann, the successful potato merchant in the North Rhineland with a Nazi past, who had his licence withdrawn by the British authorities, thus plunging hungry people for miles around into deeper hunger. Mineworkers suffered terribly from the effects of denazification when countless managers and safety inspectors were dismissed. In January 1946, forty-six miners lost their lives at Peine in Lower Saxony when their cage plummeted to the bottom of the mine. Next month at Unna near Dortmund 418 died in a coal dust explosion. Here too was a lamentable absence of experienced safety inspectors and rescue crews; safety expert and ex-Nazi Dr Stodt was even temporarily released from prison to oversee the rescue and it was his decision not to immediately cap the mine that led to the rescue of a few more miners to add to the fifty-seven who survived.

The situation was worsened further, and the reputation of the British irreparably tainted, by the shameful and hideous state of the internment camps and the lengthy incarceration of inmates without trial. While not in any way comparable with the atrocities perpetrated in Nazi concentration camps, things were, nevertheless, bad enough for a House of Commons committee to condemn the camps, to point out how inconsistent they were to the aim of turning Germans more to a British way of life, and how they flew in the face of attempts to restore "the rule of law and the professed abolition of Gestapo methods". Operating under the cloak of justice and security, No. 74 Combined Services Detailed Interrogation Centre (CSDIC) opened its doors at Bad Nenndorf near Hanover in June 1945. Spa rooms and cubicles were converted into cells to imprison and interrogate suspected former Nazi and SS members to prevent them, apparently, from fomenting resistance to the British occupation. What became known as a torture centre did not stop with German victims; suspected Russian communists and infiltrators were held and violated here. Prisoners arrived in cattle trucks. The alacrity with which the British assumed this odious role must have surprised even the Russians, so swiftly did it follow on from the ceasefire. All the usual tortures were on the agenda: sleep deprivation, exposure to extreme cold, whipping, unnecessary and casual surgery, beatings, threats against wives and children, starvation, thumb screws and shin screws. There were three deaths occasioned by the depravities endured and some inmates on release weighed less than a hundred pounds.

The Winckler Baths at Bad Nenndorf where the torture centre was established. (Fatelessfear)

Of the alleged ex-Nazis many turned out not to be German, never mind Nazis. Some were from eastern European countries offering to spy for Britain so were tortured to establish that their intended defection was genuine; one had spent time in a Gestapo prison and declared that he never had to endure there anything like what he suffered at the hands of the British. The deaths and illnesses prompted an investigation in early 1947 and a court martial, worldwide publicity, and closure followed. The camp doctor, a Captain Smith, was cleared of manslaughter at the court martial but was convicted at a secret hearing of neglect and dismissed from the army. One of the interrogators, Lieutenant Langham, denied mistreatment and was acquitted. The commandant, Colonel Robin Stephens or 'Tin Eye Stephens', ex MI5, was tried in camera and had all charges against him dropped, allowing him to resume work with MI5.

Not surprisingly, the Germans saw this as indicative of the worst of British behaviour, reminiscent of the British colonial days; accordingly they questioned how they could assume to be credible re-educators. Soon after the closure of Bad Nenndorf a new purpose-built interrogation centre was opened near Gütersloh to house, not Nazis, but suspected Russian spies. Most of the interrogators were recruited from ex-Bad Nenndorf staff.

Unfortunately Bad Nenndorf was not the only scenario in which the victorious British army mislaid their moral compass and with it the post-war high moral ground they aimed to occupy in the face of Nazi depravities and in their role as self-styled re-educators of the German along so-called British lines of decency and civilized behaviour.

Of the estimated eleven million German POWs immediately after the war about 7.6 million were captured by the Western allies; just under half of the eleven million

Despite the six years of bitter fighting which lay behind him, James Morgan-Jones, a major in the Royal Artillery, could not have been more specific about the spectacle in front of him. "It was," he reported, "one of the most disgusting sights of my life."

Curled up on a bed in a hospital in Rotenburg, near Bremen, was a cadaverous shadow of a human being. "The man literally had no flesh on him, his state of emaciation was incredible," wrote Morgan-Jones. This man had weighed a little over six stones (38kg) on admission five weeks earlier, and "was still a figure which may well have been one of the Belsen inmates." At the base of his spine "was a huge festering sore", and he was clearly terrified of returning to the prison where he had been brought so close to death. "If ever a man showed fear, he did," Morgan-Jones declared.

Adolf Galla, 36, a dental technician, was not alone. A few beds away lay Robert Buttlar, 27, a journalist, who had been admitted after swallowing a spoon handle in a suicide attempt at the same prison. He too was emaciated and four of his toes had been lost to frostbite.

CSDIC, a division of the War Office, operated interrogation centres around the world, including one known as the London Cage, located in one of London's most exclusive neighbourhoods.

As horrific as conditions were at the London Cage, Bad Nenndorf was far worse. Last week, Foreign Office files which have remained closed for almost 60 years were opened after a request by *The Guardian* under the Freedom of Information Act. These papers, and others declassified earlier, lay bare the appalling suffering of many of the 372 men and 44 women who passed through the centre during the 22 months it operated before its closure in July 1947.

They detail the investigation carried out by a Scotland Yard detective, Inspector Tom Hayward, following the complaints of Major Morgan-Jones and Dr Jordan. Despite the precise and formal prose of the detective's report to the military government, anger and revulsion leap from every page as he turns his spotlight on a place where prisoners were systematically beaten and exposed to extreme cold, where some were starved to death and, allegedly, tortured with instruments that his fellow countrymen had recovered from a Gestapo prison in Hamburg. Even today, the Foreign Office is refusing to release photographs taken of some of the "living skeletons" on their release.

Ian Cobain, *The Guardian,* 17 December 2005

Three Russian girls still wearing their slave labour uniforms photographed soon after their arrival at No.17 Displaced Persons Assembly Centre, Hamburg Zoological Gardens. (Sgt. J. Mapham/ No. 5 Army Film & Photographic Unit)

were released within a year but 1.5 million never made it home and no one knows—or admits to knowing—what happened to them. We can only speculate. POWs were covered by the Geneva Convention and Hague Conventions but the classification of the captured enemy was made not so simple, on the instigation of the British. Captives were classified as Surrendered Enemy Persons or Disarmed Enemy Persons: 4.2 million were POWs but the remaining 3.4 million were designated either SEPs or DEPs and outside the protection of the Red Cross and the Geneva and Hague conventions; in effect they were stripped of their combat status, their POW status and the protective rights which came with that status. The International Red Cross had neither mandate nor jurisdiction within the barbed wire which detained SEPs and DEPs. The British effectively swerved the treatment they would have received as POWs and ignored the statutory minimum daily calorie levels (2,000–3,000 per day). They were earmarked for long-term slave labour: the British were the original proposers of the plan to help clear up the damage of the German towns and cities. Such inhumane and uncivilized treatment of prisoners of war normalized brutality and may well have contributed to the xenophobia and mutual hostility exhibited by both British and Germans in the early days of the BAOR.

On denazification the Allies had to give in. A report by the military government published 15 January 1946 criticized the denazification programme, saying, "The present procedure fails in practice to reach a substantial number of persons who supported or assisted the Nazis." It was then decided to involve the Germans, so in March 1946 the Law for Liberation from National Socialism and Militarism (*Befreiungsgesetz*) was enacted, transferring responsibility for denazification to the Germans. Each zone had a minister of denazification. On 1 April 1946, a special law established 545 civilian tribunals under German administration (*spruchkammern*), with a staff of 22,000 of mostly lay judges, too many for all the staff themselves to be thoroughly investigated and cleared before taking office. They had a case load of 900,000. The official aim of denazification was now rehabilitation rather than solely punishment. Efficiency improved, but rigour declined. Many people now had to fill in a new form, called a *meldebogen* (replacing the hated *fragebögen*), and were given over to justice under a *spruchkammer*, which assigned them to one of five categories:

V.   Persons Exonerated (*Entlastete*). No sanctions.
IV. Followers (*Mitläufer*). Possible restrictions on travel, employment, political rights, plus fines.
III. Lesser Offenders (*Minderbelastete*). Placed on probation for 2–3 years with a list of restrictions. No internment.
II. Offenders: Activists, Militants, and Profiteers, or Incriminated Persons (*Belastete*). Subject to immediate arrest and imprisonment up to ten years performing reparation or reconstruction work plus a list of other restrictions.
I.   Major Offenders (*Hauptschuldige*). Subject to immediate arrest, death, imprisonment with or without hard labour, plus a list of lesser sanctions.

Creative ways of reducing the workload and increasing 'efficiencies' were rife: unless their crimes were serious, members of the Nazi Party born after 1919 were exempted on the grounds that they had been brainwashed; disabled veterans were also exempted; more than 90 percent of cases were judged not to belong to the serious categories and therefore were dealt with more expediently. More 'efficiencies' followed; the tribunals accepted statements from third parties regarding an accused's involvement in Nazism: whitewashing or *Persilscheine,* nicknamed after Persil. To add to this blatant adulteration of justice, Nazis were buying and selling denazification certificates on the black market; Nazis found guilty were often punished with fines assessed in reichsmarks, which were worthless. In Bavaria the denazification minister, Anton Pfeiffer, reinstated 75 percent of officials the Americans had dismissed, and reclassified 60 percent of high-ranking Nazis. The denazification process had lost all credibility; hostility was being aimed against Germans who helped administer the tribunals. Something had to give—and it was the Russians who inadvertently and indirectly provided a way out.

By 1948, the Cold War was heating up and the US, not unreasonably, became increasingly more exercised about the threat posed by the Eastern Bloc. The remaining cases were tried through summary proceedings with the result that many judgments had questionable judicial value. Finally, in 1951 the provisional West German government granted amnesties to lesser offenders and ended the programme. After all, as we have seen, for the Americans Operation Paperclip had already creamed off and imported the best scientific minds, Nazis or otherwise.

The British government was, in time, more concerned about rebuilding the German infrastructure and her economic prowess, despite having short-sightedly bombed it to destruction, than about expending time and money on pursuing Nazi criminals. From 1942 the British evolved a plan assigning a number junior civil servants to head the administration of liberated territory in the rear of the armies, with rigorous powers to remove from their post, be it public or private anyone suspected of having Nazi sympathies.

In October 1945, the only way to rebuild a working legal system, and given that almost all German lawyers had been members of the Nazi Party, the British decided that half of the German legal civil service could be staffed by 'nominal' Nazis. In the industrial sector the British began by being lenient about who owned or operated businesses, but they became more stringent when they expanded the role of trade unions, affording them decision-making powers over ex-Nazi industrialists.

So, by prudence and pragmatism, the British and BAOR avoided being swamped by denazification investigations. They went further when they streamlined the process by ordaining that no one need fill out the *fragebögen* unless they were applying for an official position. In January 1946, the British handed over their denazification panels to the Germans.

Fraternization has always been one of the less malicious byproducts of war, and of the occupation of foreign lands. In the context of the BAOR it specifically involved British troops (usually men) forming relationships (usually 'romantic') with German civilians (usually women). Immediately after the war such relationships were strictly *verboten*. Forbidding the mixing of BAOR personnel with the population they had come to occupy was intended as a form of punishment for the Germans, a British slap on the collective German wrist; it was seen as the right thing to do to shun Germans, women and children in particular; it was an unlikely occupation of the high moral ground: consorting with the recent enemy was just not right, and it was certainly not going to happen—or so that was what was thought.

A German woman gags as she walks past the exhumed bodies of some of the 800 slave workers murdered by SS guards near Namering, laid out so that townspeople can see the work of their Nazi leaders. (Cpl Edward Belfer/ Nara)

US soldiers show German civilians from Weimar corpses at Buchenwald concentration camp.

The Americans led the way. Eisenhower and the Department of War established a strict non-fraternization policy during the war; American Army radio chimed with this and GIs stationed in Germany were constantly regaled with hysterical slogans such as "Don't make friends!", "Be suspicious!" and "Every German girl is a funeral march!" The handbook published to help GIs get around Germany shrieked: "Your attitude toward women is wrong—in Germany. You'll see a lot of good-looking babes on the make there. German women have been trained to seduce you. Is it worth a knife in the back?"

Issued in September 1944, the Allied ban on fraternization "to counter insidious and dangerous propaganda" was intended to fend off attacks and ostracize the perpetrators of the Third Reich's war crimes. The idea of collective guilt was pedalled extensively, as troops were told that "practically every German was part of the Nazi network" and that included children and women. Even casual mingling attracted a fine of $65; hence asking a German girl out became known as the '$65 Question'.

But the 'good-looking babes' prevailed. The US State Department and Congress, probably starting to appreciate the impracticality of the regulations, took a less draconian line and the policy was gradually lifted. In June 1945, the prohibition against speaking to German children was eased and in July, speaking to German adults in special circumstances was permitted. In September, the policy was abandoned in Austria and Germany altogether.

Nevertheless life was never going to be easy for the fraternized woman in Germany. In the early days of the occupation, US soldiers were forbidden to pay maintenance for a child they admitted having fathered: to pay was deemed "aiding the enemy". Later, the obligations of fatherhood became entirely voluntary as maintenance was only payable if the alleged father admitted paternity. Prejudice, discrimination and exclusion followed many of these thousands of women for the rest of their lives, especially those whose child or children were of mixed race.

Marriages between US soldiers and Austrian women were not allowed until January 1946 and with German women until December 1946. Then the floodgates opened: by 1949 around 20,000 German war brides or 'GI brides' had immigrated to the United States. To put it all into context, though, 60,000 British women travelled west from the UK to be with their GI husbands in the US after Congress passed the GI Bride Act in December 1945.

Back in Germany, many US troops had always had a real problem reconciling the devastated cities and starving people they encountered with the official belligerent images they had seen in Frank Capra's training film *Your Job in Germany*. The policy of non-fraternization was first announced to many of the soldiers in this 12-minute-49-second film: "The Nazi party may be gone, but Nazi thinking, Nazi training and Nazi trickery remains. The German lust for conquest is not dead … You will not argue with them. You will not be friendly ... There will be no fraternization with any of the German people."

The propaganda film was produced by the US Army Signal Corps and written by Theodor Geisel, better known to us as Dr. Seuss. It has been criticized as a "bitter and angry anti-German propaganda film" that characterized the post-war German mind as "diseased".

Military command received the first requests from GIs wanting to marry their *fräuleins* in the autumn of 1944, but were refused. Twenty-three-year-old Robert J. Lauenstein of St Louis was the first GI granted permission to marry a German, in November 1946.

Babies and love are not the only products of fraternization: fraternizing with the enemy also brings with it the perennial problem of sexually transmitted infections (STIs, then called venereal disease or VD) among military personnel. Indeed, the fear of driving STIs underground and thereby reducing the numbers of those seeking treatment leading to more contagion, probably influenced the eventual decision to lift the ban on fraternization. Contracting an STI was sure evidence that fraternization had occurred; disclosure was an offence so non-disclosure was bound to increase as a result, the very opposite to what the epidemiologista, health authorities and the US government wanted. Solution: eliminate the offence. An example of the prevalence of STIs comes with the Scottish regiment at the end of 1945 which had 108 men suspected of having an STI out of 800 men. Infection in itself was not an offence but failing to report it was. To try and stem the epidemic, the infected were paraded throughout the town on a Sunday morning, allegedly so that German girls could identify sources of contagion and make a more informed decision as to whom they slept with.

Obviously, sex was available for sale through the numerous brothels operating in Germany. In Hanover they were located in a street running parallel to the five platforms of the station and were known as 'Platform Six'. Hamburg, with its red-light district—the Reeperbahn—turnstiled at either end, was probably the biggest brothel in the world. In 1953, sex in Germany (depending on what you wanted) cost the equivalent of a tin of Nescafé, a bar of chocolate or perfumed soap and sometimes just two cigarettes. By the mid-fifties capitalism intruded and this had risen to twenty cigarettes and by the mid-sixties it was strictly cash only.

Initially, the BAOR followed suit when they criminalized fraternisation. British troops were forbidden to visit Germans, exchange gifts, shake hands, dance, take walks or talk to them. The War Office advised caution, declaring stuffily with typical British reserve in the handbook it distributed to soldiers stationed in Germany that German women "will be willing, if they can get the chance, to make themselves cheap for what they can get out of you". There are records of incorrigible officers

Above: Nothing much had changed when this photo was taken in 2005. It shows the entrance to Herbertstraße off the Reeperbahn; the red sign to the right of the gate reads, "No entrance for juveniles under 18 years of age and women." The large cigarette advert reads literally, "For more foreplay." (Andreas Strasser)

Left: A working *fräulein* displays her wares. (Juliana da Costa José Juhu)

being court-martialled and reduced to the ranks for their intemperance and intransi-
gence, and of wayward other ranks being incarcerated and demoted. An RSM serving
in Austria was broken to private by a court martial for responding to an Austrian
girl who asked him the time. But men and women will be men and women, be they
British or German, so in spite of the ban and the criminality of it all, soldiers still
consorted with local women. Montgomery, Eisenhower's counterpart, was against the
ban, and it was lifted in July 1945. At one point, with disarming logic, he wrote to
Churchill asking how we were to integrate the Germans back into Europe if we were
not allowed to talk to them.

"I have some 20 million German civilians in the British Zone. You cannot re-educate such a number of people if you never speak to them." He later says in his mem-
oirs: "It was a great relief to get this matter settled. I had never liked the orders which
we had to issue; but it was Allied policy."

Montgomery's four messages to British troops regarding non-fraternization,
issued between March and September 1945, show how his policy gradually lightened,
starting from a strict ban on any contact with the 'enemy' as attitudes changed and
the British realized that ostracizing the Germans was not conducive to rebuilding
Germany into a strong economic force. This message from April 1945 is unequivocal:
"In streets, houses, cafés, cinemas etc, you must keep clear of Germans, man, woman,
and child, unless you meet them in the course of your duty. You must not walk out
with them, or shake hands, or visit their homes, or make them gifts, or take gifts from
them. You must not play games with them or share any social event with them. In
short you must not fraternize with Germans at all."

On 5 June he wrote: "We cannot expect the soldier to go on snubbing little children; he must be allowed to give full play to his natural kindly instincts. We do not
want the German children to regard the British soldier as a kind of queer ogre."

On 12 June, Churchill issued his second personal message to the German people of
the British zone, clearly at pains to explain the ban to them. The message is patroniz-
ing and, to our ears, verges on the comedic: "Again, after years of waste and slaughter
and misery, your Armies have been defeated. This time the Allies were determined
that you should learn your lesson—not only that you have been defeated, which you
must know by now, but that you, your nation, were again guilty of beginning the war.
For if that is not made clear to you, and your children, you may again allow your-
selves to be deceived by your rulers, and led into another war ... You are to read this to
your children, if they are old enough, and see that they understand. Tell them why it
is that the British soldier does not smile."

On 25 September, Montgomery announced the full relaxation of the ban, with the
provisos that no allied soldiers were to be billeted with Germans or allowed to inter-
marry. The ban on inter-marriage prevailed for a further eighteen months or so, and

the first marriages between British soldiers and German women went ahead in early 1947 "in cases where the reasons for marriage are good and there is no security objection". Approval had to be sought from a senior military commander and the couple had to endure a number of strict conditions, including a 'cooling-off' period of six months from the date of application, when the man had to return to the UK on his own as part of his annual leave. About 10,000 British men serving with the armed forces or the civilian Control Commission married German women between 1947 and 1950.

"When I first got engaged to my wife we weren't allowed to get married. And then it was announced in the House of Commons that people could get married to Germans ... And when I applied I was told I couldn't get married. They didn't accept the parliamentary ... what had gone through parliament they didn't accept.

"I had to apply to, well fundamentally at that time the local commander, who was a brigadier I think from memory; this was in the Control Commission of course. And he said I couldn't get married, and in fact ... I knew him quite well ... he said, 'Look I'd much sooner you married a wog, rather than marry a German. They're [Germans] quite terrible people.' I said, 'I don't agree.' Anyway I got fed up with this. I knew the thing had gone through Parliament and I had a neighbour who was an MP ... my parents had a neighbour who was an MP, so I went home and told him the story.

"Anyway he said he'd take it up, and when I got back to Germany there was a big notice on my desk: 'Here is your authority to get married. God help you.' So I started to sort things out, and then I was told that the Germans were still operating under the laws of the Third Reich, so the Third Reich forbade German citizens to marry foreigners. So I had to take a car and a driver and go all over the place in Germany to sort out the legal situation. I finished up at what amounts to ... what would be the equivalent over here ... a sort of district legal office ... and I sat down with the German civil service lawyers and we thrashed out a method of doing this.

"When we'd sorted it out I went back and applied and got married in a German registry office. I set up a sort of ... established notice of how to do it and this was circulated. I was told three thousand other couples married in that year ... based upon what I'd negotiated with the Germans."

Mr J. M. G, Thexton, interview 7 November 2007. (IWM sound archive)

At the end of the day, local men between the ages of sixteen and sixty were in short supply due to German casualties and the hundreds of thousands still detained in POW camps. Only the war disabled remained and there was neither help nor sympathy for heroes. Women aged between twenty and forty outnumbered men by 160 to 100. The victorious armies could not have failed to appear attractive, particularly with their jubilation, offerings of food, cigarettes, stockings, 'a good time' and the like. Small wonder that German women demanded "Where are our men?"

Rape is a facet of all wars, and has been since time immemorial although it is inconsistently reported or confessed to, usually for spurious reasons such as 'bad for morale' or 'men will be men'. No doubt

Miss Von der Heyde leads children in a physical education class at a British Army of the Rhine study centre at Iserlohn. (Gunner V. A. Headebrouck, No 5 Army Film & Photographic Unit / IWM)

there were will have been instances of rape during the early occupation of Germany by British troops but records are curiously sparse, to say the least. No such embarrassment accompanies the French and the Russians whose barbaric behaviour is often mitigated by the undeniable fact that their own women were subject to violation by the Germans on the way to Moscow or during the Nazi occupation of France. As for the Americans, around 200 GIs were executed for rape committed in Britain and in the occupied countries but none was ever punished in Germany, despite 284 convictions.

As time went by British soldiers and airmen integrated more and more with the Germans, forsaking the regimental or squadron mess and venturing downtown into the bars and pubs and the local fairs (*schützenfest*) where they rubbed shoulders with German men and women. Long-term romance and casual sex were the inevitable consequences of this liberation, as was binge-drinking the relatively strong pilsners on a prodigious scale. The inevitable street violence often ensued and became an issue that threatened the good relations between British and Germans. Moreover, fraternization was not always a bed of roses, as the truth emerged of some soldiers' undisclosed wives and children back home. By 1955, over 68,000 illegitimate children had been fathered by occupation soldiers, with many never to learn who their fathers were.

9. BRITISH FAMILIES ON THE RHINE

For the most part, postings to BAOR regiments were accompanied, that is wives and children went to Germany with their men. Wives—and increasingly husbands of female personnel—and children were, therefore, an integral part of the BAOR and of the BAOR experience. Although often ignored or glossed over, the British family on the Rhine is an important and integral element of the BAOR story.

BAOR 'settlements' in Germany—there was as many as 140 locations over the BAOR period spread throughout northwestern German and West Berlin—have been described as "a bubble of home comforts in a foreign land", as "a British archipelago in the middle of a German sea", as "a cocoon of Britishness" where the streets often have British names redolent of imperious British history. Such were the comforting amenities laid on for troops and their dependants in and around army quarters (or SFAs, service family accommodation), and on camps. Schools, shops (NAAFI, YMCAs and Toc H), adult education, cinemas, the messes, support organizations, sport, equestrian pursuits, hospitals, doctors, dentists, inter-unit competitions, Sunday lunches, barbeques, balls, bingo, raffles, and churches were all provided for the use and delectation of the men, women and children of the BAOR. Indeed, so comprehensive and British were the facilities and social activities that a family never had to venture away from that insulated cocoon 'outside the wire' that was army life in BAOR, although many would admit that this was a missed opportunity of the first order as German culture, society, scenery, the people and their history were and are experiences not to be missed. At any one time or another on average up to 50,000 military personnel were stationed in Germany, for a total of around 200,000-plus British men, women and children.

However, despite all the facilities and ex-patriot Britishness of it all, there was no escaping the sobering fact that the military families were, just as much as their husbands (or wives), living on the front line in the unpredictable and potentially lethal Cold War, embedded as they were in the first line of defence. While this perilous situation may not have normally exercised the families unduly, allowing them to get on with life, it nevertheless was a fact that in the event of a significant Warsaw Pact push, they all had a life expectancy of about eight hours and, in the worst scenario, would have been incinerated. The best they could expect was to be taken prisoner after forty-eight hours when the BAOR surrendered, and who knows what terror and indignities that would have brought, all part of the so-called 'futile sacrifice'. A stark example of the fragility of the peace was the fraught Cuban Missile Crisis in 1962, when families in Cologne were ordered to prepare for evacuation.

The British on the Germans, the Germans on the British

What did the British think of their German hosts and what did the Germans think of their British guests? We have seen how an initial policy of non-fraternization soon elided into a period in which British troops were able to consort with and marry German women if they so wished. The early prohibition was predicated on a perceived need to punish and, if not exclude the Germans from this new version of German society controlled by the British, then keep them mindful of who were the victors and who were the vanquished in post-war Germany. The subsequent liberal attitude was predicated on the new policy to integrate Germany and the Germans into a population that contributed to the strength of a new post-war Europe with a robust economy and a rearmament programme which reinforced the allies' defence against the Warsaw Pact forces massed against them just along the road behind the Iron Curtain.

The BAOR, therefore, was anxious to foster positive and productive relations with the Germans now that the stigma, negativity and unpopularity of acting as an army of occupation had been, in theory at least, consigned to the past. But numerous obstacles, initially stood in the way of this hoped-for *entente cordiale*, or *herzliches verständnis* as a German might say. They included still-fresh memories of the recent war and its fallout in which many British lost family or had them return home disabled for life, in which many British were blitzed out of their homes, in which the Germans had won for themselves a reputation for repellent cruelty on an industrial scale, systematic ethnic-cleansing and supreme and odious arrogance. Then there was the innate British xenophobia and insistence on monolingualism; the stereotypical German portrayed as a goosestepping thug in British media and culture; the behaviour of and German response to British servicemen behaving badly in a foreign land, energized by boredom and animated by alcohol; the superbly provisioned 'little Englands' established by the British which virtually obviated any real need to step 'beyond the wire' and integrate and communicate with the Germans on their doorstep.

In the very early days the Germans were, for the most part, also resentful at being occupied, and at the British insistence that they, the British, were eminently well qualified to re-educate the Germans back to a kind of normality, a British version of normality at that; they were disturbed to see their towns overrun by sometimes inebriated foreign soldiers who thought nothing of whisking their girls and women (their potential wives) off their feet; they were outraged by the agro-economic depredations caused by the often abrupt appropriation of vast tracts of sometimes ecofriendly German land churning it into quagmires and muddy fields for the delectation of tank crews and for the exclusive use of British artillery, armour and infantry; they were equally depressed when the services commandeered their homes and hotels, evicting owners and tenants and failing to return them to the German housing stock when they fell empty as they sometimes did.

Miss Heather Maxwell with some of the children attending a BAOR study centre at Iserlohn. (Gunner V. A. Headebrouck, No 5 Army Film & Photographic Unit / IWM)

In a country that had so recently lost much of its housing stock the pressure put on civil accommodation by the British was not only unwelcome but a cause of huge resentment. To give some examples, Wuppertal had lost 153,000 homes, Krefeld lost 40 percent of its housing, rendering 90,000 people homeless; 85 percent of Cologne was flattened, 90 percent of Hanover. And then came the floods of refugees, displaced persons from the east, statuses negotiated at Yalta and Potsdam: in the British-occupied *Land* of Schleswig-Holstein nearly three million refugees poured in seeking accommodation alongside the 1.6 million residents. The population of Lower Saxony grew from 4.5 million in 1939 to 6.7 million in 1947. In the British-occupied Rhineland alone 100,000 refugees were being held in 200 camps By February 1947 906,000 refugees had turned up in North Rhine-Westphalia. And then along came the BAOR with their families. In total, the allies requisitioned over 16,000 houses, 11,000 plots of land, 679 barracks, over 13,000 flats, over 8,000 single rooms, 1,200 hotels and 600 restaurants. The price of war, particularly the price of a war lost, never ends when the shooting stops. Occupation and economic regeneration has extensive social implications for the defeated population—and housing/ garrisoning was one of the more significant and far-reaching.

Nothing much changed very quickly: in 1951 there were still 60,000 requisitioned buildings on BAOR's books. Insensitive allocation exacerbated the dire situation further; it was not uncommon, for example in Lübeck, for a senior NCO with wife and one child to be given a requisitioned German house and home with six bedrooms, a large garden, a nanny and daily help. Such extravagant luxury did not last but it took until 1956 for it to be eradicated.

According to a 1951 report in *Rheinische Post*, the number of people with claims against the German government due to requisitioning stood at 3.5 million: "For six years these people had been waiting for the return of either their homes or other property like furniture requisitioned by the Allies." *Rheinische Post* estimated that the number of displaced persons as a result of requisitioning made up as much as 6.8 percent of the entire German population.

The area around Bad Oeynhausen, the original headquarters of the BAOR until 1954, gives a glaring example of high-handed and thoughtless requisitioning. According to Lance-Corporal Gordon Cox, RAMC Bielefeld, in Roy Bainton's account: "'Baddo' as it was called, was a very pleasant spa ... Unfortunately the 10,000 'Deutschers' had been evicted from their nice little town to make way for 1,000 officers and 2,000 other ranks who acted as clerks, batmen, drivers, runners and every kind of dogsbody to the officers."

Peter Speiser takes up this woeful story: "Barbed wire fences separating the British from the Germans in Bad Oeynhausen were only removed in 1951, when seventy hectares of requisitioned land, including the spa gardens, were handed back to the Germans. Nonetheless, forty per cent of all available living space in the town continued to be requisitioned by the BAOR. By the time the British headquarters at Bad Oeynhausen were finally closed, the physical and economic damage caused by the BAOR was considerable. The town had lost, 'apart from [the damage caused by] the thirty-two minor and medium fires, the Protestant church, a 750,000 DM bathing house and four private residences', all of which had been requisitioned by the British. A local newspaper article outlined how under British 'rule', the largest thermal spring in Europe had remained closed to anyone but the BAOR and how the only public building in town accessible to the German public had in fact been a public lavatory. The entire train station with all ticket offices and waiting rooms was reserved for 'the handful of British tourists', while the last remaining church bells were not allowed to ring for German but only for English services."

In 1952 no less than 125 square miles of North Rhine Westpahlia had been appropriated for British military use, not including the land on which requisitioned houses, hotels and hostels stood on. On top of this was the land required for four new airfields, a training area for Dutch troops, an air-to-ground firing range, land for an additional 10,000 Belgian troops and space for the Canadians. The airfield in the Niederrhein region alone in 1951 entailed the eviction of 151 farms at a cost of 6 million deutschmark. Aircraft noise and road congestion were other gripes as the

RAF swooped down on Germans and bombed bombing ranges to destruction such as those on Heligoland which the British had summarily evacuated in 1945 for use as a permanent bombing range. The evacuation, however, followed Operation Big Bang in which the British in April 1948 exploded 7,000 tons of munitions in what was described as "the greatest non-nuclear explosion in history". The intention in what would have been more aptly named Operation Overkill was to destroy German fortifications and submarine docks on Heligoland; in the event, barely a tenth was eradicated, but the point—destroying Prussian militarism—was made. Meanwhile endless convoys choked the autobahns; accidents and manoeuvre-damage just added to the turmoil. And to the mutual dissatisfaction.

> "When one looks back, it is almost hard to believe the scale of the field exercises [FDX] that took place in those halcyon days before the three gremlins of 'track mileage', 'flying hours', and 'damage control' all entered our military vocabulary. Huge areas of the German countryside were given the '443 treatment' by the staff (the official Army Form used to designate the civilian countryside as suitable for rape and pillage), and then all hell was let loose as we exercised our rights to defend NATO. The sights of great convoys of military vehicles clogging the autobahns for miles, the crazy patterns of tank and APC tracks carving their way through fields and villages, and the crowds of harassed burghers wringing their hands in despair as their homes and barns were 'requisitioned' by the military—all these were familiar to us on an all too regular basis."
>
> Colonel P. V. Panton OBE

We have noted how excessive drinking and extended periods of boredom contributed to the friction and tension between occupier and occupied. Examples of the consequences of this potent cocktail are reported in the *April 1954 Public Safety Report* for the Westphalia area. In one a German civilian died from his injuries and one British soldier was stabbed in the back and seriously wounded. The same report listed for July 1954 nine cases of malicious damage by British personnel, ten common and four indecent assaults and one case of rape by servicemen, as well as seven brawls involving service personnel and four thefts. Typical was the incident in Hamburg in May 1954 when "a soldier grabbed a German woman by the breast and hip and offered her five DM for permission to have sexual relations with her". Gallantry this was not. According to one soldier who served in Brunswick in 1957, one of the best pastimes "at which they could pass many hours" was the "Goodwill

Mission" where troops would go down to the railway station and foment "a tremendous brawl with the locals", frequently involving hundreds at a time and sometimes lasting all night.

Other ranks were not the only miscreants. In the summer of 1952, an officer drove his tank into the garden of a restaurant in Lower Saxony after having been refused a drink. £1,000 worth of damage later, the officer was severely reprimanded, although he is alleged to have been congratulated by his commanding officer for showing initiative. In another incident a British major was apprehended by the military police in Hamburg after crashing his car into a German taxi and kicking the driver in the stomach, while "under the influence of drink". On such occasions the German press always had a field day deriding BAOR's efforts to exhibit the values of Western democracy.

Frighteningly, children were not exempt from hostile action: a local German government report tells how a primary school-aged German child was attacked by a group of English children aged ten to fourteen. "The children stole his purse, tied his hands and feet together and threw him into a pond where he was saved from drowning by a passer-by."

Between July 1955 and July 1956, 302 British soldiers broke the law in Lower Saxony including two cases of manslaughter, seventeen cases of rape and 130 cases of theft. North Rhine-Westphalia interior ministry figures for the same period show an increase in the number of crimes by British soldiers. Inebriation incidents in bars and restaurants showed a rise from eighteen to twenty-eight while burglaries rose from thirty-one to forty-eight. Sexual offences by British soldiers increased from fifteen to eighteen; violent crimes committed by British soldiers rose from forty-six to sixty.

Other, often quite petty, incidents at the highest level increased the mutual animosity. One such case was the spat over fox-hunting in Wolfenbüttel. The time-honoured British way of fox-hunting had been banned in the Federal Republic, a ban which after 1949 also applied to Allied troops in Germany. A local British unit had demanded an exemption supported by the British Resident and Captain Lord Blandford of the Life Guards'who penned a letter highlighting the potential damage the hunting issue threatened to cause for Anglo-German relations in general. After all, fox hunting was "taking place in a large number of European countries and the only reason it was outlawed in Germany was due to Hermann Goering's decision in 1937". Diplomatic this was not and it would have cut no ice. Furthermore, the good Lord added petulantly that British officers had spent "considerable amounts of time and money to buy and train their dogs and would, due to this unfriendly and short-sighted action of yours, receive preciously little joy and amusement in return". But 'joy and amusement' was

German crime statistics of 1957 revealed just how favourably the behaviour of British troops compared to that of the Americans. Between July 1956 and September 1957 US troops in Bavaria committed eight murders, 319 cases of grievous bodily harm and 136 cases of robbery as well as 207 cases of rape. The corresponding figures for the British area of Lower Saxony were zero murders, twenty-seven cases of grievous bodily harm, nine cases of robbery and twenty-three cases of rape. Corresponding figures for North Rhine-Westphalia, which was also predominantly under British control, were zero murders, sixty-four cases of grievous bodily harm, twenty-six cases of robbery and thirty-six cases of rape. The overall number of offenders in [US army-occupied] Bavaria during this period was 714, whereas in Lower Saxony this figure was remarkably low with only twenty-six British offenders. In North Rhine-Westphalia there had been 195 delinquents during the period in question. The collection of data by the Federal Government continued and in March 1957, the German Ministry of Foreign Affairs revealed a list, compiled by the Länder, of incidents between the Allied Forces and the local population for the eighteen months ending December 1956. For Baden-Württemberg, Bavaria, Hesse and Rhineland-Palatinate (the areas in which French and American troops were stationed) the total was 1,051; in contrast to this North-Rhine Westphalia, Lower Saxony, Hamburg and Schleswig-Holstein (the British and Belgian area) totalled a mere 137 incidents.

P. Speiser

to follow after all when the German official concerned, Herr Lieberkuehn, subsequently complained that British troops had hounded him after he refused to grant the exemption and when on the night following the refusal Herr Lieberkuehn's house came under attack by "heavy and very heavy" British pyrotechnic devices. The excuse given by the British was that the flares were an ovation to their commanding officer to celebrate Battle of Hastings Day and that they had accidentally targeted the wrong house. The CO lived nowhere near Herr Lieberkuehn.

Despite it all both the British and the German authorities did strive to improve Anglo-German relations, both with single servicemen and with families, encouraging joint sports events, joint Christmas celebrations, guided coach tours, excursions and other ways to open up the many cultural experiences and treasures inherent in Germany. The *Westdeutsches Tageblatt*, was able to report in 1952 some signs of success. However, there remained a number of difficulties which we seem to have met before, including the typical Anglo-Saxon lethargy which prevents the English from actively looking for new friends and learning new languages as well as the German tendency to come across as too friendly and therefore give the impression of ingratiation.

By and large, British newspapers, magazines and comics did nothing to help. The endless diet of war films too played their part but did not promote the xenophobia and stereotypes typical of the press to such an extent. Indeed, there was something of a gulf between the stereotypical portrayal of Germans, for example in *The Wooden Horse* (1950) and *The One that Got Away* seven years later which, like *The Dambusters* (1955) and the American *Stalag 17* (1953) were more balanced and nuanced. Servicemen in Germany in the sixties and seventies may well have grown up reading *The Valiant* comic in which an ever-triumphalist and short-fused Royal Marine Captain Hurricane destroyed countless Germans almost single-handedly every Monday—Germans whose command of their native language was restricted to a few short exclamations of incredulity: *Donner und Blitzen! Gott in Himmel! Hande hoch! Raus!* and *Feuer!* spring to mind. The Beaverbrook newspapers in particular dished up a relentless diet of anti-German sentiment and hostility.

Relations were further strained by the German miracle, the *Wirtschaftswunder*, 'the Miracle on the Rhine', in which the German economy had been rapidly and efficiently restored and revivified. Despite the obvious relatively comfortable standards enjoyed by many army families, the comparative standards of living between Germans and English both in the UK and in the BAOR were eyed enviously by British servicemen and civilians alike, thus adding to the social and economic tensions between the two races in Germany. Veteran journalist Fyfe Robertson may have put his finger on it when he suggested in 1955 in the *Picture Post* that the British were perhaps not working as hard as the Germans, not giving "a fair day's work for a fair day's pay". The same indolence continues to blight British productivity today: back in the 1950s and 1960s this truth will have hurt the casual reader.

Over time, things did improve, immeasurably. Friendships were forged on all levels, languages were learnt, culture was imbibed and mutual respect and understanding flourished. Regimental magazines took a more cultural line becoming more like tourist guides, extolling the treasures to be experienced beyond the wire, near and far.

Housing

As noted, army families lived in army quarters on what was known as the army patch. At the beginning of the post-war occupation the British simply moved in, requisitioned German houses and flats, evicted the occupants and moved their dependents in. There was an obvious initial shortage of accommodation which lasted until 1961 at least, necessitating in some garrisons in the temporary use of caravans.

This 1961 newspaper caption gives the details: "Bought by the army to help relieve the shortage of married quarters in Germany: one of 200 30-ft. caravans made by the Bluebird Company. They have been carefully planned in close consultation with the War Department and are being delivered at a rate of twenty a week."

The Royal Signals' magazine, *The Wire*, added more in June 1962, describing five of the caravans allocated to 1st Signal Regiment at Cluvental Barracks in Verden: "The caravans themselves bear little resemblance to the popular conception of a 'towing van' of the type towed by the average medium-sized family car. These are the 'super-de-luxe' models, which really live up to the description of homes on wheels. Externally, they are attractively furnished in pale blue, while the interiors are fully and tastefully furnished. The appointments include a double bedroom with fitted wardrobe, bathroom with bath and separate lavatory, kitchen complete with sink unit, refrigerator and electric cooker, and a bright lounge equipped, among other things, with a settee which converts easily into a double bed. French windows from the lounge open on to a pleasant verandah with wrought-iron rails. Curtains, carpets and all furnishings are of modern design, while wall-fitted electric fires in each room and insulated walls keep the caravans snug and warm against the rigours of the North German winter."

In time, sufficient purpose-built married quarters were built as required. Quarters in Germany tended to be of a much higher quality and specification than those left behind in the UK: they had, for example, central heating, fridges (instead of larders), a big cellar, a shower and outside lighting.

Food

A Guide for Families in Germany (including 41 Garrison, Hook of Holland), is part of a fascinating BAOR publication dated May 1954 produced for newcomers to life with the BAOR. It gives a detailed insight into how the army accommodated, catered and cared for and entertained army families posted to BAOR, nine years after the end of World War II, "produced with the object of answering many queries which will arise during your stay in Germany". The somewhat censorious introduction betrays the rather regimented and rigid aims and scope, and the flavour: "Please remember that the total British service families in Germany include some 12,000 wives and over 12,000 children, which is comparable with a British town in England of the size of Windsor. Yet this married population is scattered over an area which is equivalent to England and Wales. You therefore must realize that distance and transport facilities which have such a bearing on our daily life in UK are very different out here. We are continually examining the problems of your wellbeing, but we cannot transport your home town facilities to your own military station out here. Help us by giving constructive ideas and we will do our best to help you."

Right: British soldiers queue for tea at NAAFI Mobile Canteen No. 750 beside the Brandenburg Gate, Berlin. This van was the first mobile NAAFI to operate in Berlin, 16 July 1945. (IWM)

Below: The NAAFI building in Osnabrück, February 2010. (O. S. Meyer)

The guide featured some intriguing frequently asked questions, and comments:

Q: Is it safe to eat food obtained from German shops or in German restaurants?

A: Yes. Certain worm diseases are commoner in Germany than at home, but can be prevented by thorough cooking or food.

Q: Is German ice-cream safe?

A: Do not let your children eat ice-cream, except from NAAFI sources. German ice-cream is not subject to British medical supervision.

Q: Is it safe to drink milk and cream from German sources?

A: Fresh German milk and cream is not controlled by the military medical authorities, who cannot therefore guarantee that its consumption will not lead to serious infectious disease. Pasteurized milk and cream, bottled in the dairy and sold in sealed bottles is the safest on offer to the German public. Milk distributed in churns or cans is liable to contamination in distribution and cannot be considered safe unless boiled before consumption. All milk can be made safe by boiling.

German cake fillings made from milk or cream should not be eaten as they are liable to contamination in distribution and cannot be sterilised after manufacture.

The Family meat ration: The meat issue is one of the most important items in the family ration, and no effort is spared to ensure distribution on the basis of 'fair share'. Complaints received often indicate a lack of knowledge of the system of supply, and the method by which the Quartermaster computes his families' entitlements. Frequently the causes of complaints can be attributed to the actual cooking process.

The NAAFI

The Navy, Army, Air Force Institutes (NAAFI) was the hub of all life for British military personnel, or so it seemed at times. NAAFI ran canteens and clubs for service families for relaxation, socialization and entertainment in peace and in war. It runs launderettes, restaurants, clubs, bars and cafes, but the real NAAFI experience came with the NAAFI supermarket. NAAFI was established in 1921. The outbreak of World War II saw NAAFI mushroom with the number of employees rising from 8,000 to a peak of 110,000 and the number of trading outlets growing from 1,350 to nearly 10,000.

Health Care

The health needs of BAOR personnel and families were catered for in a two-tier system which reflected the NHS system in the UK. Primary care (GP) was dealt with by military medical centres while secondary care took place in a number of military hospitals, BMH (British Military Hospital) Iserlohn, Berlin, Hanover, Rinteln, Hamburg, Hostert and Münster. In 1946 inoculation against small-pox, typhoid and typhus was required before travel to Germany while the Schick test was used for children and adults up to the age of thirty to check if they were susceptible to diphtheria.

BMH Berlin closed 1994. The building, on Heerstraße, is now a civilian hospital called Paulinen Krankenhaus. Rudolph Hess was a visitor here with a full floor blocked off and dedicated to his care. BMH Hamburg is still a military hospital, but for German forces. It is now called Bundeswehrkrankenhaus Hamburg. Erich von Manstein (1887–1973), German commander of the Wehrmacht, was held here, heavily guarded and with his own squad of German nurses, *Schwesternunterkunf*.

BMH Iserlohn started off as No. 6 British General Hospital in 1946. From 1978 to 1993 it was NATO 31 Field Hospital in support of I (BR) Corps. It was refurbished in 1985, during which time staff worked at Münster. It reopened in 1991 as a 200-bed hospital when BMH Münster closed. BMH Hanover was closed and then mobilized as 32nd Field Hospital to Saudi Arabia during the Gulf War in 1990.

> "[BMH Hanover] was a vast modern hospital compared to the ancient British edifices, with wards for servicemen and their families, hence women's and children's wards. They were run as other military wards, except that we did no cleaning or 'bumping' because the German fraus came in each day for that. They also cleaned the nurses' single rooms on the top floor of the main hospital block. These were well furnished with such luxuries as bedside lights and dressing tables! Heaven, after shared billets and severe austerity in the UK ... We were hugely impressed with the double glazing, unheard of back home, and the quantity and quality of all hospital equipment, particularly instruments and capacious autoclaves. In theatres we had some German surgeons, and I remember that the talented German woman eye surgeon refused to don surgical gloves to operate ... All the things we now take for granted were new and exciting—Wiener Schnitzels and biergartens, tiergartens and tea dances, where young German men were forbidden to fraternize with us. Outdoor musicians, and department stores selling perlons [nylons] and lacy lingerie galore! Anything frivolous was still in short supply in blighty."
>
> Stephanie Lowe, Qaranc 1955

Parts of BMH Rinteln buildings and grounds are now being used by the German charity Lebenshilfe. BMH Hostert started life as a Franciscan monastery. During the Nazi era the site was used to implement euthanasia. After the war and in British hands, it became BMH Hostert until the early 1960s when it was converted to Kent School. BMH Oldenburg was built in 1935 for the Wehrmacht, as Standort-Lazarett (Static Military Hospital). It was taken over by British forces as BMH Oldenburg at the end of the war. Returned to the Germans in 1950 as the Städtischen Krankenanstalten, it is today the Klinikum Oldenburg. BMH Wuppertal was in 1953 was The Queen Elizabeth the Second British Military Hospital, Wuppertal. Today it is the Bethesda Krankenhaus.

The British Forces Post Office (BFPO)

The purpose of the British Forces Post Office (BFPO) is "to provide an efficient and effective postal and courier service in order to sustain the fighting power of UK armed forces worldwide". The numbers for BAOR bases were Berlin: 30, Bielefeld:

Guide to families proceeding to BAOR, August 1946

Baggage Arrangements [1cwt = 50.8kg]
The scale of total baggage allowed for families proceeding to B.A.O.R. is as follows:
Wives of Lt.-Cols. and above . . . 8 cwts.
Wives of Majors, Captains and Subalterns . . . 6 cwts.
Wives of Warrant Officers . . . 5 ½ cwts
Wives of other ranks . . . 4 ½ cwts.
Each child . . . 1 ½ cwt. and pram.
Bicycles may be sent within the above entitlement.

Accompanied Baggage
Of the total quantity allowed, families may actually take with them not more than 1 cwt. in respect of the wife and ½-cwt. plus a folding pram in respect of each child. Baggage required on the journey should be packed separately from that not required.

Money
You will be allowed to exchange £5 for yourself and £5 for each of your children into B.A.F.S.V.s (British Armed Forces Special Vouchers). This is the only type of currency which you will be able to spend in Germany and English money will be useless to you. Arrangements have been made for this exchange to be made before you embark.

Domestic Animals
Domestic animals, such as dogs and cats, cannot at present be taken in military transports and any application for permission for them to accompany you will be refused.

39, Celle: 23, Dulmen: 44, Elmpt: 35, Fallingbostel: 38, Gütersloh: 47, Hamburg: 30, Hameln: 31, Herford: 15, Hohne: 30, Mönchengladbach: 19, Münster: 17, Osnabrück: 36, Paderborn: 22, Rheindahlen: 40 and Sennelager: 16.

Education

In 1946 a survey found that if families accompanied their military personnel spouses the total number of children aged between 0 and 15 would be about 6,000 with the greatest requirement being for primary education. In June 1946 the Cabinet agreed that families should join serving personnel as part of Operation Union, so long as the education the children received was "at least equal to" that they would have received in the UK. Somewhere now had to be found to educate the children and someone had to be found to teach them. British Families Education Service BFES was established by the Foreign Office in cooperation with the War Office and Ministry of Education. The first school to open was Prince Rupert School in Wilhelmshaven.

Local education authorities were required to help recruit teachers for work in the schools in the British zone with an estimation that 200 would be required. Two thousand applied and the first teachers arrived in Germany in November 1946. British families started arriving from August 1946 onward and small informal schools were set up in some areas before official BFES schools opened. The first official BFES schools opened in early 1947, mostly in requisitioned buildings including private houses.

In the 1951/2 the service was taken over by the army and became the Service Children's Education Authority (SCEA) and, in 1989, renamed the Service Children's School (SCS) before adopting its current name the Service Children Education (SCE) in 1997. At this point there were fifty-eight schools worldwide, thirty-nine of which were in Germany. In 2013 schools began closing in Germany after it was announced British forces would no longer be stationed in the country.

A report in the *Times Educational Supplement* by By Martin Whittaker, 10 March 2006, gives an insight into BAOR schooling and life as a service school teacher: "In the last round of Ofsted inspections, around 40 per cent of these schools were declared outstanding. They are well-resourced and get a significant budget for continuing professional development. And some schools are working with the Qualifications and Curriculum Authority at the leading edge of curriculum design   They do not have the extremes of poverty and affluence that afflict UK state schools, and class sizes are small.

"But there are other challenges: pupil mobility is high, averaging around 70 per cent in primaries ... Marlborough First School in Osnabrück, northern Germany, has seen the turnover rate of children increase in the last few years since the Army has been on active service in the Middle East. A recent inspection report described the school as outstanding, providing a crucial anchor for its community during a time of particular disruption and anxiety for service families ... It means we have to have strategies in place, good induction procedures for the children, and high-quality assessment.

"Karen Palin, a Year 3 teacher ... likes the pupil-teacher ratio—her class has 17 children: 'Every class has a teaching assistant and there's strong special educational needs support ... you're given an equivalent military rank and are housed accordingly—an NQT [newly qualified teacher] is ranked the same as a captain. It doesn't confer authority, and you won't get saluted. But there are perks such as first-class travel as you go up the ranks. And you do get access to the officers' mess ... So while an NQT would get a £19,161 starting salary, they also get an annual overseas recruitment allowance of £3,916 and a tax-free transfer grant of £1,373. In addition they also receive a tax-free cost of living addition, which varies depending on marital status and family size. They also get rent-free accommodation for the first five years, and subsidised heating and electricity.'"

The Northern Ireland Factor

Any feelings that BAOR wives felt of isolation and vulnerability in Germany were heightened by those of separation caused by The Troubles raging in Northern Ireland from 1969 to the mid-1990s. The UK government's commitment to the province required a continuous series of rotating six-month tours carried out using all sectors of the British army. That, of course, entailed the postings of BAOR personnel to Northern Ireland on an ongoing basis, causing additional stress and anxiety for many of the wives left in Germany. To improve deteriorating morale, popular British television shows were for the first time beamed out to British bases from 1975. The unexplained absence of this facility had been a constant cause of complaint for over two decades. Apart from boosting morale, English-language TV had the effect of reducing drink-driving to negligible levels as personnel and their families stayed at home watching the TV.

To exacerbate matters, in 1979 the Provisional Irish Republican Army (IRA) and the Irish National Liberation Army (INLA) both initiated campaigns to internationalize their campaigns of terror which entailed extending their reach to threaten British army personnel serving in Germany. Here is their catalogue of terror:

- 1979: Richard Sykes, then British Ambassador to the Netherlands, and his Dutch valet, Krel Straub, were killed in a gun attack in Den Haag, Netherlands; four British soldiers were wounded when the IRA detonated a bomb under a bandstand in Brussels, as British army musicians were getting ready to perform.

- 1980: Colonel Mark Coe, was shot dead by an IRA unit outside his home in Bielefeld.
- 1981: The INLA claimed responsibility for exploding a bomb outside the British consulate in Hamburg; that November the INLA claimed responsibility for exploding a bomb at the British army base in Herford, West Germany; one British soldier was injured.
- 1987: Thirty-one people were injured on 23 March 1987 after a 300lb car bomb exploded near the officers' mess at JHQ Rheindahlen. The casualties comprised twenty-seven West Germans—mostly West German military officers who had been invited to spend an evening with their British counterparts—and four British.
- 1 May 1988: there were two separate attacks on the same day against British military personnel in the Netherlands. At Roermond a gun attack resulted in the death of one RAF member (Ian Shinner, 20) and badly injuring a second soldier. Police said that at least 23 bullets were fired into the vehicle. In Nieuw Bergen, a bomb placed under the car of four RAF soldiers exploded while they were parked outside a disco, killing two of them (John Miller Reid and John Baxter) and injuring the other two. These attacks were seen as revenge for the SAS killings of the three IRA volunteers in Gibraltar two months previously. (All BAOR civilian vehicles carried conspicuous British military licence plates which identified them as British army- or RAF-owned and driven. This practice was eventually ended when British-owned cars assumed standard British civilian plates, a move that was criticized for putting British tourists at risk as their cars were indistinguishable from the cars of military personnel.
- August 1988: A British sergeant-major was shot dead at Ostend, Belgium.
- July 1989: A British soldier was killed by an IRA booby trap bomb in Hanover.
- 7 September 1989: Heidi Hazell, 26, the German wife of British army sergeant Clive Hazell, was murdered at the wheel of her British-registered, dark-blue Saab outside her married quarters in Unna-Massen, a Dortmund suburb. Heidi had been shot "in the belief that she was a member of the British army garrison at Dortmund".
- 28 October 1989: IRA members opened fire on the car of RAF corporal Mick Islania as he and his family returned to the car from a petrol station snack bar in Wildenrath. Also in the car were his wife Smita and their six-month-old daughter Nivruti. Corporal Islania was hit by multiple rounds and died instantly; his daughter was killed by a single shot to the head. Smita Islania survived. The IRA expressed regret for Nivruti's death and claimed its members did not know she was in the car.

- 27 May 1990: Nick Spanos and Stephen Melrose were Australian tourists shot dead in the Netherlands by the IRA; the terrorists claimed to have mistaken them for off-duty British soldiers and called the shooting "a tragedy and a mistake". The car used by Spanos and Melrose had British number plates.
- 1 June 1990: Major and Mrs Michael Dillon-Lee had been to a party before he was gunned down. Major Dillon-Lee, 35, was battery commander of the 32nd Heavy Regiment Royal Artillery stationed in Dortmund.
- 28 June 1996: Three Mk 15—homemade 'barrack busters' to the IRA—mortar bombs were launched by IRA volunteers at Quebec Barracks, Osnabrück, from a Ford Transit van; each bomb contained more than 180lb of explosive. Ironically, the van had been modified by a former British Army REME engineer, Michael Dickson, who built the launch platform and aimed the tubes at the barracks. Two of the bombs fell short of the perimeter fence and failed to explode, but the third went off twenty yards inside the base, leaving a crater near a petrol pump. There were 150 soldiers inside the facility at the time, but none was injured.

Entertainment

Individual units put on a plethora of entertainment and sporting events— garrison welfare clubs, amateur dramatics, equestrian activities, garrison saddle clubs, polo, Weser Vale bloodhounds, sailing etc—throughout the year. In addition there was BFBS radio dedicated to troops and families, and there were the films screened daily by the Army Kinema Corporation (AKC), shows put on by the Combined Services Entertainment Unit (CSEU); and Boy Scouts and Girl Guides for army children.

Originally, during the war, AKC was part of ENSA. (Entertainments National Services Association). After the war, this part was hived off and became the Army Kinema Corporation under the War Office. In 1958, the headquarters of the AKC in BAOR was in Kingsley Barracks, Minden. This included the film vaults, film distribution centre, and workshops. Film distribution throughout the two circuits was both on a Monday and a Thursday when programmes were moved by road on to the cinema on the circuit. The Royal Air Force had its own independent cinema organization called Astra involving some twelve Astra cinemas on RAF bases throughout BAOR. By February 1958, there were approximately 48 cinemas operated by the AKC in BAOR. Usually, most were in barracks but Münster, for example, was not. This Globe cinema was located in the former Hauptbahnhof Kino (main railway station). For children throughout the BAOR the Saturday morning matinées were *de riguer* with endless exciting Zorro films and the like.

The Globe, Fort Prince of Wales, Deilinghoven, near Hemer, in the 1960s.

In the early days British Forces Network (BFN) provided local weather forecasts, UK news bulletins and a wireless programme every day along the lines of the BBC Light Programme.

The Combined Services Entertainment Unit put on throughout the year a regular programme of theatrical companies that visted all the main garrisons in Germany. They included plays, musicals and variety productions, many by West End companies: "CSEU aims at providing everyone in Germany with access to live theatrical entertainment at least once each month. For the amateur actor there are a number of unit and garrison theatre clubs who always welcome new talent."

The British Forces Radio/ British Forces Broadcasting Service programme that everyone remembers was *Two-way Family Favourites* broadcast simultaneously from Cologne and London with Judith Chalmers and Cliff Michelmore as presenters, with twenty million listeners in the UK and, according to the Bundespost, seven million in Germany. Sometimes the two-way became three- or four-way when other British army locations such as Cyprus and Hong Kong were added to the mix. Just as famous was Bill Mitchell—or Uncle Bill—with his unmissable *Tales of Big Wood.*

There was also a TV version from the mid-1950s for which strict guidelines dictated the type of people soldiers could request music for: only wives and other (very) close family could be the dedicatees: fiancées and girlfriends were excluded.

Uncle Bill in his office at BFBS in Cologne.

Other programmes made especially for BAOR personnel and their dependants were interspersed with popular programmes out of London such as *The Archers*.

The Services Sound and Vision Corporation (SSVC) was established in 1982 from the merger of the Services Kinema Corporation (SKC) and the British Forces Broadcasting Service (BFBS) to "entertain and inform Britain's Armed Forces around the world"; its activities include the British Forces Broadcasting Service with its radio and television operations, SSVC cinemas, the British Defence Film Library, and its live events arm, Combined Services Entertainment (a successor to ENSA).

EPILOGUE: THE LAST POST

The BAOR was wound up in 1994 after the fall of the Berlin Wall, the lifting of the Iron Curtain and the evaporation of the threat of invasion from the Soviets and the Warsaw Pact. The BAOR had come into existence some forty-nine years earlier on 25 August 1945, taking over from the British Liberation Army as an army of occupation, to suppress the defeated Germans. This role soon elided into a more productive and pragmatic function when the BAOR spearheaded, along with the Americans and French, a programme designed to expedite and foster the regeneration of West Germany as a fully functioning economic, political and military force within NATO. The strategy then was not to suppress, but to enable growth and to strengthen. At the same time, the BAOR in their zone was a vital cog in a multinational military alliance

9 November 1989, the day the wall—built 13 August 1961—came down and the beginning of the end for the BAOR. (The photo shows a part of a public photo documentation wall at the Brandenburg Gate, Berlin. The photo documentation is permanently placed in the public domain.)

Volkspolizei at the official opening of the Brandenburg Gate, 22 December 1989. (S/Sgt Lee Cochrane / U.S. DoD)

whose presence in Germany, specifically on the North German Plain, was designed to deter, delay and defend against any incursion by Warsaw Pact forces into West Germany. This was, in effect, the BAOR's essential role in the Cold War which was 'fought' from the late 1940s to the early 1990s.

The British army maintained its presence in the new Germany for many years from 1994 as the 25,000-strong British Forces Germany (BFG). The defence of the West, training and family lives continued, but there has been a slow but inexorable programme of station closures, to culminate in 2019/20 with the final closure of barracks at Paderborn, Sennelager, Gütersloh and Bielefeld. The British army will continue to exercise and train on the plains and in the forests and hills of Germany but its job as an army garrisoned there on permanent deployment is certainly done. What is equally certain is that the BAOR's experience as a significant Cold War protagonist between 1945 and 1994 and what it learnt from its service in Germany will continue to provide a supremely professional basis and examplar for the British army of the future, whatever the role and wherever the theatre.

SOURCES

Aldrich, R. J., 'Intelligence within BAOR and NATO's Northern Army Group', *Journal of Strategic Studies* 31, 2008

_____, 'Strategy and Counter-Surprise: Intelligence within BAOR and NATO's Northern Army Group', University of Warwick thesis 2008

Alter, P., 'Building Bridges: The Framework of Anglo-German Cultural Relations after 1945' in Jeremy Noakes et al (eds.), *Britain and Germany in Europe, 1949–1990*, Oxford, 2002

anon, *The British Army: A Pocket Guide 3rd Edition*, R & F Military Publishing, 1991

_____, *A Woman in Berlin*, London, 2004

Bainton, Roy, *The Long Patrol: The British in Germany, 1945–1990*, Edinburgh, 2003

Barker, E., *Britain in a Divided Europe, 1945–1970*, London, 1971

Barrass, G. S. 'The Great Cold War: A Journey Through the Hall of Mirrors', Stanford Security Studies, 2009

Bellis, M. A., *The British Army Overseas*, 2001

Biddiscombe, P., 'Dangerous Liaisons: The Anti-Fraternization Movement in the U.S. Occupation Zones Of Germany And Austria, 1945-1948', *Journal of Social History*. 34 (3) 2001, pp. 611-647

Biddiscombe, P., *The Denazification of Germany 1945–48*. Stroud, 2006

Blaxland, G., *The Regiments Depart: A History of the British Army, 1945–1970*, London, 1971

Blume, P., *BAOR: The Final Years 1980–1994*, Tankograd British Special No. 9006, Erlangen, 2007

Breitenstein, B., *Total War to Total Trust. Personal Accounts of 30 Years of Anglo-German Relations*, London, 1976

Buckley, J., *Monty's Men: The British Army and the Liberation of Europe*, New Haven, 2013

Calleo, D. P., *The German Problem Reconsidered: Germany and the World Order, 1870 to the Present*, Cambridge, 1978

Chambers, P. (ed.), *Called Up: The Personal Experiences of Sixteen National Servicemen, Told By Themselves*, London, 1955

Chrystal, P., *Roman Military Disasters*, Barnsley, 2015

_____, *Rome: Republic into Empire - Battles of the 1st Century BCE*, Barnsley, 2018

_____, *Wars and Battles of Ancient Greece*, Stroud, 2018

_____, *Wars and Battles of the Roman Republic*, Stroud, 2015

Clark, D. F, *Stand By Your Beds!, A Wry Look at National Service*, Glasgow, 2006

Clifton, G., *The Experience of Education of the Army Child*, PhD thesis, Oxford Brookes University, 2007

Clifton, G., 'Making the Case for the BRAT (British Regiment Attached Traveller)', *British Educational Research Journal* 30, 2004, pp. 457-62

Cohen, M., *Fighting World War Three from the Middle East: Allied Contingency Plans, 1945–1954*, London 1997

Cornish, P., 'The British Military View of European Security, 1945–50', in Anne Deighton (ed.), *Building Postwar Europe*, Basingstoke, 1995, p. 70.

Crowfoot, C.R., *The Combat Composition of the Armed Forces of the Union of Soviet Socialist Republics* [Боевои Состав Вооруженные Силы Союз Советских Социалистических Республик 1988 гг.], version 3.0.0, 1988

Davies, R. M., 'British Orders of Battle & TO&Es 1980–1989' v 4.3

Deighton, A. 'Cold-War Diplomacy: British Policy Toward Germany's Role in Europe, 1945-49', in I. D. Turner (ed.) *Reconstruction in Post-War Germany: British Occupation and the Western Zones,* Oxford, 1989, pp. 15-36

_____, *Britain and the First Cold War*, Basingstoke, 1990

_____, *The Impossible Peace: Britain, The Division of Germany and the origins of the Cold War*, Oxford, 1993

_____, (ed.), *Building Postwar Europe*, Basingstoke, 1995

_____, 'Minds, not Hearts: British Policy and West German Rearmament' in C. Haase (ed.) *Debating Foreign Affairs. The Public and British Foreign Policy since 1867*, Berlin, 2003, p. 78.

DeVirgilio, L., *see* Vieuxbill, L.

Dewar, M., *Defence of* the Nation, London, 1989

Diefendorf, J., *In the Wake of War: The Reconstruction of German Cities after World War Two*, Oxford, 1993

Dockrill, S. *Britain's Policy for West German Rearmament, 1950–1955,* Cambridge, 1991

_____, 'Retreat from the Continent? Britain's Motives for Troop Reductions in West Germany, 1955–1958', *Journal of Strategic Studies* 20, 1997, pp. 45-70

Dorman, A. M., *Defence under Thatcher*, London, 2002

_____, *The Nott Review*, Institute of Contemporary British History, London, 2002

Dunstan, S. *Centurion Main Battle Tank: 1946 to Present,* owners' workshop manual

Durie, W., *The British Garrison Berlin 1945–1994: A Pictorial Historiography of the British Occupation*, Vergangenhertsverlag, Berlin 2012

Edmonds, J. E., *The Occupation of the Rhineland 1918–29*, London, 1987

Elsom, S., *Remembering Osnabrück: The British Garrison 1945–2009*, Osnabrück, 2008

Evgenios, M., 'After the War and after the Wall: British Perceptions of Germany following 1945 and 1989', *University of Sussex Journal of Contemporary History* 3, 2001

Falcon, R., 'Images of Germany and the Germans in British Film and Television Fictions' in Harald Husemann (ed.) *As Others See Us. Anglo-German Perceptions*, Frankfurt, 1994, p. 18

Faringdon, H., *Strategic Geography: NATO, the Warsaw Pact and the Superpowers 2nd Edition.* London, 1989

Farquharson, J., 'Emotional but Influential: Victor Gollancz, Richard Stokes and the British Zone of Germany, 1945-9', *Journal of Contemporary History* 22, No. 3, 1987, pp. 501-519

Flemming, T., *The Berlin Wall: Division of a City*, Berlin 2013

Foley, M., *The British Army of the Rhine after the First World War*, Stroud, 2017

Fossey, M., *Unsung Heroes: Developing a Better Understanding of the Emotional Support Needs of Service Families*, 2012

Flieshart, J., 'Bridging Cultures during the Cold War: The British Army of the Rhine's (BAOR) Dortmund Garrison and their German Civilian Workers', *Landscapes* 15, 2014, pp. 132-142

Forty, G., *They Also Served: A Pictorial Anthology of Camp Followers Through the Ages*, Spelhurst, 1979

Fraser J. H., *Yalta 1945: Europe and America at the Crossroads*, Cambridge, 2010

French, D., *Army, Empire, and Cold War: The British Army and Military Policy, 1945–1971* Oxford, 2012

_____, *The British Army of the Rhine, Middle East Land Forces, and Conventional Deterrence: 1948 to 1956*, Oxford, 2012

_____, *The British Army of the Rhine's Doctrine for Nuclear War*, Oxford, 2012

_____, *The British Army of the Rhine and the Nuclear Battlefield*, Oxford, 2012

French, P, *BAOR Boarding School 1948–1959*, Andover, 2014

Friedrich, J., *The Fire: The Bombing of Germany, 1940–1945*, New York, 2006

Funder, A., *Stasiland: Stories from Behind the Berlin Wall*, London, 2011

Gander, T. J., *Britain's Armed Forces Today: 3 British Army of The Rhine*, London, 1984

_____, *Encyclopedia of The Modern British Army*, 3rd Edition, Patrick Stephens Ltd., Yeovil, 1986

_____, *The Modern British Army: A Guide to Britain's Land Forces*. Patrick Stephens Ltd., Yeovil, 1988

_____, *Infantry of the Line*. London, 1988

_____, *The Royal Engineers*, Littlehampton Book Services Ltd, 1985

Gibson, C, 'Children of the Regiment', *Practical Family History*, March 2007

_____, 'Minors on the March', *Ancestors*, September 2008

_____, 'Following the Drum', *Family History Monthly*, September 2009

_____, 'Married Quarters: Then and Now', *AFF Families Journal*, Winter 2009.

_____, *Army Childhood: British Army Children's Lives and Times*, Oxford, 2012

Gibson, M, *How the Army Wife Gained Status and a Voice in 1982*, Canterbury, 2002

_____, *The Day the War Ended: VE Day 1945 in Europe and Around the World*, London, 1995

Gimbel, J., 'On the Implementation of the Potsdam Agreement: An Essay on U.S. Postwar German Policy', *Political Science Quarterly* 87, 1972, pp. 242-269

Goedde, P., *GIs and* Germans, London, 2003

Griffin, R., *Challenger 1: Main Battle Tank Vol. I*, Photosniper No. 9, Lublin

_____, *Challenger 1: Main Battle Tank Vol. II*, Photosniper No. 11, Lublin

_____, *Chieftain Main Battle Tank: Development and Active Service from Prototype to Mk.11*, Photosniper No. 7, Kagero Publishing, Lublin 2013

Haase, C., 'In Search of a European Settlement: Chatham House and British-German Relations, 1920–55, *European History Quarterly* 37, 2007, pp. 371-397

Headquarters, Department of the Army, Washington, DC, *The Soviet Army: Operation and Tactics*, Field Manual No. 100-2-1

Hennessey, P., *Having it So Good: Britain in the Fifties*, London, 2006

Herrmann, K. (ed.), *Coping with the Relations: Anglo-German Cartoons from the Fifties to the Nineties*, Osnabrück, 1988

Herz, J. H., 'The Fiasco of Denazification in Germany', *Political Science Quarterly*, 63, 1948

Heuser, B., 'Britain and the Federal Republic of Germany in NATO, 1955-1990', in J. Noakes (ed.) *Britain and Germany in Europe, 1949–1990*, Oxford, 2002

Heuser, B., 'Victory in a Nuclear War? A Comparison of NATO and WTO War Aims and Strategies', *Contemporary European History* 7, pp. 311–327, 1998

Hickman, T., *The Call-Up: A History of National Service*, London, 2004

Hoffenaar, J. (ed.), *Blueprints for Battle: Planning for War in Central Europe, 1948–1968*, University of Kentucky, 2012

Horne, A., *Back into Power, A Report on the New Germany*, London, 1955

Hughes, R. G., '"Don't let's be beastly to the Germans": Britain and the German Affair in History', *Twentieth Century British History* 17, Vol. 2, 2006, pp. 257-283

Isaacs, J. *Cold War*, London, 1998

Isby, D. C., *Armies of NATO's Central Front*, London, 1985

_____, *Weapons and Tactics of the Soviet Army*, 2nd ed., London, 1988

Janowitz, M., 'German Reactions to Nazi Atrocities', *American Journal of Sociology* 52, 1946, pp. 141-146

Johnson, B. S., *All Bull: The National Servicemen*, London, 1973

Kershaw, I., *The End: Hitler's Germany 1944–45*, London

Kirchoff, A. *British Infantry Brigade Berlin*, Tankograd Publishing, 2005

Kirkpatrick, I., *The Inner Circle*, London, 1959

Kramer, M. N., 'Civil–military relations in the Warsaw Pact, The East European component', *International Affairs* 61, 1984–85

Kynaston, D., *Austerity Britain, 1945–51*, London, 2007

_____, *Family Britain, 1951–57*, London, 2009

Laber, T., *British Army of the Rhine: Armoured Vehicles on Exercise*, Concord Publications, 1992

le Carré, J. *The Spy Who Came in from the Cold*, London 1963

Lee, S., 'Deterrence and Defence of Central Europe: The British Role from the Early 1980s to the end of the Gulf War', PhD thesis, King's College, London, 1994

_____, *An Uneasy Partnership: British-German Relations between 1955 and 1961*, Bochum, 1996

_____, *Victory in Europe? Britain and Germany since 1945*, Harlow, 2001

Lesley-Dixon, K. *Northern Ireland: The Troubles: From the Provos to The Det, 1968–1998*, Barnsley, 2018

Lewis, G. J., *Flugplatz Gütersloh 1937–1987: A Short History*

Lewis, W. J., *The Warsaw Pact: Arms, Doctrine, and Strategy*, Cambridge, Mass., Institute for Foreign Policy Analysis, 1982

Lewkowicz, N. *The German Question and the Origins of the Cold War*, IPOC, Milan, 2008

Longyear, M. (ed.), *A New Life: Some Pupils' Accounts of the First Full Year in the Life of Prince Rupert* School, Germany, 2007

_____, *Prince Rupert School: The Creation of a Boarding School for Service Families in Post-war Germany*, 2006

Lowe, K., *Savage Continent: Europe in the Aftermath of World War II*, London, 2012

MacDonagh, G., *After the Reich: From the Liberation of Vienna to the Berlin Airlift*, London, 2007

Mackintosh, M., 'The Evolution of the Warsaw Pact', International Institute for Strategic Studies, 1969

Major, P., 'Britain and Germany: A Love–Hate Relationship?', *German History*, 26, 4, 2008, pp. 457-468

Mallinson, A., *The Making of the British Army: From the English Civil War to the War on Terror*, London, 2009

Mann, A., *Comeback: Germany 1945–1952*, London, 1980

Mason, T., *Sport and the Military, The British Armed Forces, 1880–1960*, Cambridge, 2010

Mastny, V. *A Cardboard Castle?: An Inside History of the Warsaw Pact, 1955–1991*, Budapest, Central European University Press, 2005

Mawby, S., *Containing Germany: Britain and the Arming of the Federal Republic*, Basingstoke, 1999

Mann, Golo, *The History of Germany Since 1789*, London 1987, p. 812

May, T., *Military Barracks*, Oxford, 2002

McAdams, A. J., *East Germany and Détente*, Cambridge, 1985

_____, *Germany Divided: From the Wall to Reunification*, Princeton University Press, 1992

McInnes, C. J., *Hot War, Cold War: The British Army's Way in Warfare 1945–1995*, London, 1996.

_____, 'BAOR in the 1980s: Changes in Doctrine and Organisation, *Defense Analysis* 4, 1988, pp. 377-394

McMahon, R. J., *The Cold War: A Very Short Introduction*, Oxford, 2003

McNish, R., *Iron Division: The History of the 3rd Division 1809–2000*, 3rd ed., London, 2001

Meehan, P., *A Strange Enemy People, Germans under the British, 1945–1950*, London, 2001

Michail, E., 'After the War and after the Wall: British Perceptions of Germany following 1945 and 1989', *University of Sussex Journal of Contemporary History* 3, September 2001

Miscamble, W. D., *From Roosevelt to Truman: Potsdam, Hiroshima, and the Cold War*, Cambridge, 2007

National Archives, FO 1030/174, *Marriages with ex-enemy nationals*

Noakes, J. (ed.), *Britain and Germany in Europe, 1949–1990*, Oxford, 2002

Noakes, L., *Women in the British Army: War and the Gentle Sex, 1907–1948*, London, 2006

Pawley, M., *The Watch on the Rhine: The Military Occupation of the Rhineland, 1918–1930*, 2008

Peedel, W., *Encyclopedia of the Modern Territorial Army*, Patrick Stephens Ltd, 1990

Persico E. J., *Roosevelt's Secret War*, New York, 2001

Peterson, E. N., *American Occupation of Germany*, Detroit, 1977

Pimlot, J. (ed.), *British Military Operations 1945–1984*, New York, 1984

Piorkowski, Jerzy, *Miasto Nieujarzmione*, Warsaw, Iskry, 1957

Pronay, N., 'The British post-bellum Cinema: a survey of the films relating to World War II made in Britain between 1945 and 1960', *Historical Journal of Film, Radio and Television* 8, 1988

Public Information Services BAOR, *The British Army in Germany And Berlin: Its Organization, Role, Equipment and Way of Life*, London, 1984

Ramsden, J., 'Re-focusing 'the People's War': British War Films of the 1950s', *Journal of Contemporary History* 33, 1998

_____, *Don't Mention the War, The British and the Germans since 1890*, London, 2006

Reinisch, J., *The Perils of Peace: The Public Health Crisis in Occupied Germany*, Oxford, 2013

Roberts, G., *Stalin's Wars: From World War to Cold War, 1939–1953*, Yale University Press, 2006

_____, 'Stalin at the Tehran, Yalta, and Potsdam Conferences', *Journal of Cold War Studies* 9, 2007, pp. 6-40

Robinson, M. P., *The Royal Armoured Corps in the Cold War 1946-1990*, Barnsley, 2016

Royle, T., *The Best Years of Their Lives, The National Service Experience 1945–1963*, London, 2002

Schönwald, M., 'New Friends—Difficult Friendships: Germany and its Western Neighbours in the Postwar Era', *Contemporary European History* 11, 2002, p. 318

Schulze, C., *The British Army of The Rhine*, Europa Militaria, Marlborough, 1995

_____, *Key Flight '89: The Last Cold War Exercise of the BAOR*, Tankograd British Special No. 9010, Erlangen, 2009

Smith, B., 'The Rules of Engagement: German Women and British Occupiers, 1945–1949', Theses and Dissertations (Comprehensive), Paper 1072

Speiser, P., *The British Army of the Rhine: Turning Nazi Enemies into Cold War Partners*, University of Illinois Press, 2016

Stafford, D., *Endgame 1945*, London 2007

Stanford, F, *Don't Say Goodbye: Our Heroes and the Families They Leave Behind*, London, 2011

Stoddart, K., *Losing an Empire and Finding a Role*, 2012

Swan, R. *British Army Transport & Logistics*, London 1991

Tankograd Publishing. The series (in both English and German) gives a brief overview of each subject and focuses on the vehicles used in BAOR. Excellent pictures, many from field exercises with vehicles camouflaged as if for war:

9001	*British Infantry Brigade Berlin*
9003	*BAOR The Early Years 1945-1979*
9006	*BAOR The Final Years 1980-1994*
9010	*Key Flight '89: The Last Cold War Exercise*
9014	*FV432 Armoured Personnel Carrier*
9015	*FV432 Variants*
9018	*British Nuclear Artillery*
9020	*Challenger 1 Main Battle Tank*
9022	*Cold War Exercise Spearpoint '80*
9023	*Conqueror Heavy Gun Tank*
9025	*AT 105 Saxon*
9026	*British Cold War Military Trucks*
9027	*Stalwart High Mobility Load Carrier*

Taylor, D., *Chieftain Main Battle Tank 1966 to present: An insight into the design, construction, operation and maintenance of the British Army's Cold War-era Main Battle Tank*, owners' workshop manual, Sparkford, 2016

_____, *Challenger 1 Main Battle Tank 1983–2001 (FV 4030/4 Model): An insight into the design, operation and maintenance of the British Army's revolutionary Main Battle Tank*, owners' workshop manual, Sparkford, 2016

Taylor, F., *Exorcising Hitler: The Occupation and Denazification of Germany*, London, 2011

Thorne, T., *Brasso, Blanco and Bull*, London, 1998

Varns, N., 'It Started With a Kiss. Happy and tragic German-American love stories after World War II', *The Atlantic Times*, December 2005

Venning, A. *Following the Drum. The Lives of Army Wives and Daughters Past and Present*, London, 2006

Viergutz, V., *The Berlin Wall 1961–1989*. 2nd ed., Berlin 2015

Watson, G., *The British Army in Germany (BAOR and After): An Organizational History 1947–2004*, Milton Keynes, 2005

Watt, D. C., *Britain Looks to Germany: British Opinion and Policy toward Germany since 1945*, London, 1965

_____, 'Anglo-German Relations Today and Tomorrow', in K. Kaiser (ed.) *Britain and West Germany, Changing Societies and the Future of Foreign Policy*, London, 1971, pp. 203-218

_____, 'Perceptions of German History among the British Policy-Making Elite', in J. Foschepoth (ed.) *Britische Deutschland-und Besatzungspolitik 1945–1949*, Paderborn, 1985, pp. 15-25

Wayper, L., *Mars and Minerva: A History of Army Education*, Royal Army Educational Corps Association, 2004

Webster, W., 'From Nazi Legacy to Cold War: British Perceptions of European Identity, 1945–1964', in Michael Wintle (ed.) *European Identity and the Second World War*, Basingstoke, 2011

Westad, O. A., *The Cold War: A World History*, London 2017

Wettig, G., *Stalin and the Cold War in Europe*, Rowman & Littlefield, 2008

White, A. C. T., *The Story of Army Education, 1643–1963*, London, 1963

White, K., 'British Defence Planning and Britain's NATO commitment, 1979–1985', University of Reading PhD thesis

Williams, N. T. St John, *Judy O'Grady & the Colonel's Lady: The Army Wife and Camp Follower Since 1660*, London, 1988

_____, *Tommy Atkins' Children*: *The Story of the Education of the Army's Children 1675–1970*, London 1971

Williamson, C., 'Factors Affecting the Feasibility of a Warsaw Pact Invasion of Western Europe', senior honors thesis for Texas A&M University, 2008

Willoughby, J., *Remaking the Conquering Heroes: The Postwar American Occupation of Germany*, Basingstoke, 2001

Wittlinger, R., 'Perceptions of Germany and the Germans in Post-War Britain', *Journal of Multilingual and Multicultural Development* 25, 2004, pp. 453-456

Zimmermann, Z., 'The Sour Fruits of Victory: Sterling and Security in Anglo-German Relations during the 1950s and 1960s', *Contemporary European History* 9, 2000, pp. 225-243

Websites

http://24thmissile.tripod.com/
http://coldwargamer.blogspot.com/2014/04/orbat-british-1980-bg-nato-and-baor.html
http://dx.doi.org/10.1080/01402390701785443
http://forcescinemas.com/paderborn
http://movcon.org.uk/
http://powstanie-warszawskie-1944.ac.pl/gustaw_galeria.htm
http://royalsignalsmuseum.co.uk/WebSite/

http://syriainstitute.org/siege-watch/

http://theminiaturespage.com/boards/msg.mv?id=266896

http://www.birgelenvets.org/webpages/history.aspx

https://api.parliament.uk/historic-hansard/commons/1984/oct/22/the-army

https://archive.ioe.ac.uk/DServe/DServe.exe?dsqApp=Archive&dsqCmd=Index.tcl

https://catalog.archives.gov/id/541691

https://kclpure.kcl.ac.uk/portal/en/theses/deterrence-and-the-defence-of-central-europe-
-the-british-role-from-the-early-1980s-to-the-end-of-the-gulf-war(982e02d5-c46b-47a0-
acf3-8d599ee2f82e).html

http://scholars.wlu.ca/etd/1072

www.archhistory.co.uk/taca/memsmisc.html

www.armytigers.com/events/cold-war

www.auswaertigesamt.de/sid_CAB9AF7926D7E1097F51E96F42134382/EN/AAmt/
PolitischesArchiv/Uebersicht_node.html

www.baor-locations.org/24regtra.aspx.htm

www.baor-locations.org/borderpatrols.aspx.html

www.baor-locations.org/Home.aspx.htmlhttp://www.baor-locations.org/memories.aspx.html

www.baor-locations.org/nationalservice.aspx.html

www.baor-locations.org/RoyalNavy.aspx.html

www.bundesarchiv.de

www.durhamrecordoffice.org.uk/Pages/home.aspx

www.firepower.org.uk/

www.iwm.org.uk/collections-research/about/sound

www.kcl.ac.uk/kcmhr

www.orbat.info/history/volume5/518/Original%20BAOR.pdf

www.orbat85.nl/

www.orbat85.nl/documents/BAOR-July-1989.pdf

www.oxfordbibliographies.com/view/document/obo-9780199791279/obo-9780199791279-
0135.xml#obo-9780199791279-0135-bibItem-0002

www.paulchrystal.com

www.qaranc.co.uk/bmhiserlohn.php

www.re-museum.co.uk/

www.researchgate.net/publication/49310622_The_Joint_Intelligence_Bureau_Economic_
Topographic_and_Scientific_Intelligence_for_Britain's_Cold_War_1946-1964

www.rescue.org/sites/default/files/resource-file/IRC_WomenInSyria_Report_WEB.pdf

www.strategypage.com/militaryforums/567-1622.aspx#startofcomments

www.theberlinobserver.com/archive/1946V2/V2_N21_May_24.pdf

www.thinkdefence.co.uk/2016/03/nato-knew-throw-party

www.womenforwomen.org.uk

Index

Acknowledgements

My thanks go to Louie DeVirgilio (aka Louie Vieuxbill) who has been most generous with information and sources, all of which have improved this book immeasurably, and particularly to his http://baor-locations.org/Home.aspx.html. Thanks too to Catherine Holt, Assistant Curator PWRR & Queen's Museum, Dover, for permission to quote extracts from www.armytigers.com/events/cold-war. And to Kathryn Hannan, IOE Archivist, UCL Institute of Education Archives, London for help in finding me information on service schools in Paderborn. Thanks to George Cook for the fine image on page 64.

The following have also been very useful: Peter Speiser's thesis 'The British Army of the Rhine and the Germans (1948-1957)'; http://baor-locations.org.html and www.arch-history.co.uk/taca/memsmisc.html. Finally, many thanks to my brother, David Chrystal, who has provided a number of photographs showing aspects of his time serving in the BAOR; these help to give a realistic picture of BAOR life from the soldier's point of view.

About the Author

Paul Chrystal has degrees from the universities of Hull and Southampton; he is the author of around 100 books, a number of which are on military matters. He writes for a national daily newspaper and has appeared on the BBC World Service, Radio 4's PM programme and various BBC local radio stations. In the 1960s he lived in Paderborn, in what was then West Germany, for four years and attended King's School in Gütersloh; both his father and brother served in West Germany with the BAOR.

Other series titles by Paul Chrystal

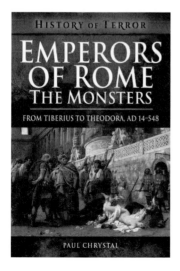

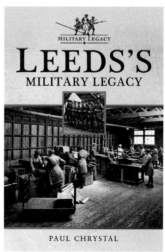

(Tigerente)